'When I walk into my kitchen, the first things I look for are my pot, my olive oil, the onion and the garlic. The pot goes on the stove, I pour in the olive oil, cut some onions and garlic and throw them in. The music of the sizzling onion and the sweet smell as the oil draws out the sugars are food for the soul.'

# GUY GROSSI my italian heart

recipes from an italian kitchen

*With Love*
*Guy 2006*

photography by Adrian Lander

illustrations by Mirka Mora

LANTERN
*an imprint of*
PENGUIN BOOKS

LANTERN

Published by the Penguin Group
Penguin Group (Australia)
250 Camberwell Road, Camberwell, Victoria 3124, Australia
(a division of Pearson Australia Group Pty Ltd)
Penguin Group (USA) Inc.
375 Hudson Street, New York, New York 10014, USA
Penguin Group (Canada)
90 Eglinton Avenue East, Suite 700, Toronto, ON M4P 2Y3, Canada
(a division of Pearson Penguin Canada Inc.)
Penguin Books Ltd
80 Strand, London WC2R 0RL, England
Penguin Ireland
25 St Stephen's Green, Dublin 2, Ireland
(a division of Penguin Books Ltd)
Penguin Books India Pvt Ltd
11 Community Centre, Panchsheel Park, New Delhi – 110 017, India
Penguin Group (NZ)
Cnr Airborne and Rosedale Roads, Albany, Auckland, New Zealand
(a division of Pearson New Zealand Ltd)
Penguin Books (South Africa) (Pty) Ltd
24 Sturdee Avenue, Rosebank, Johannesburg 2196, South Africa

Penguin Books Ltd, Registered Offices: 80 Strand, London, WC2R 0RL, England

First published by Penguin Group (Australia), a division of Pearson Australia Group Pty Ltd, 2005

10 9 8 7 6 5 4 3 2 1

Text and recipes copyright © Guy Grossi 2005
Illustrations copyright © Mirka Mora 2005
Photographs copyright © Adrian Lander 2005

The moral right of the author has been asserted

All rights reserved. Without limiting the rights under copyright reserved above, no part of this publication may be reproduced, stored in or introduced into a retrieval system, or transmitted, in any form or by any means (electronic, mechanical, photocopying, recording or otherwise), without the prior written permission of both the copyright owner and the above publisher of this book.

Design by Nikki Townsend © Penguin Group (Australia)
Cover and internal illustrations by Mirka Mora
Photography by Adrian Lander
Styling by Adair Lander; photography assistant Louise Dixon
Author photograph by Lucas Allen
Typeset in Electra LH, Nimbus Sans Novus and Bell Gothic by Post Pre-Press Group, Brisbane, Queensland
Printed and bound in China by Imago Productions

National Library of Australia
Cataloguing-in-Publication data:

    Grossi, Guy, 1965– .
    My Italian heart: recipes from an Italian kitchen.
    Includes index.
    ISBN 1 920989 30 7.
    1. Cookery, Italian. I. Mora, Mirka, 1928– . II. Lander, Adrian. III. Title.
    641.5945

www.penguin.com.au

This book is dedicated to the children.
They are a constant source of inspiration.
I see it in their eyes as we feed their hunger.

# Contents

| | | |
|---|---|---:|
| **The Beginning** | | 1 |
| **Essentials** | | 7 |
| | The Cooking Room | 9 |
| | The Tools | 10 |
| | Buying Ingredients | 11 |
| |     Meat | 12 |
| |     Fish | 14 |
| |     Fruit and Vegetables | 14 |
| | Herbs and Spices | 15 |
| | Preparations | 17 |
| **Cool Food** | | 25 |
| | Antipasto | 28 |
| | Cool First Courses | 38 |
| | Salads | 50 |
| **The Prince and the Pauper** | | 57 |
| | Pasta Fresca | 60 |
| | Zuppa | 74 |

| | |
|---|---:|
| **The Main Event** | **83** |
| Hot First Courses | 86 |
| Meat and Game | 93 |
| Fish and Seafood | 107 |
| Contorni | 114 |
| **Improvviso** | **121** |
| **Loaves and Fishes** | **135** |
| Al Fresco | 138 |
| The Feast | 144 |
| Bread | 152 |
| **Intermezzo** | **159** |
| **Sweet Things** | **171** |
| | |
| Acknowledgements | 203 |
| Index | 205 |

The Beginning

When I walk into my kitchen, the first things I look for are my pot, my olive oil, the onion, the garlic. The pot goes on the stove, the naked flame burning under it. I pour in the olive oil. As it begins to heat, the air is permeated with its beautiful aroma. I cut some onions and garlic and throw them in. The music of the sizzling onion, and the sweet smell as the heated oil draws out the sugars, is food for the soul.

The oil, the flame, the onion – these are the fundamentals of my *cucina*, and they are also a link to the past. You can trace it back for thousands of years, to the ancient Roman days. It's the base of Italian cooking, the *soffritto*. This is the beginning of the cooking, the beginning of the kitchen, the beginning of the philosophy in the kitchen.

    In my earliest memories of childhood I can see the kitchen, a place where all would come, filled with those familiar smells and the laughter of people who love each other, and with the anticipation of the flavours to come. It was perhaps here that my passion for cooking was ignited. The first day Dad took me to his work I was seven years of age. He made me peel potatoes. I got a snapshot of what a professional kitchen looked like, and as the years progressed I found my own place, a spot that I loved. I wasn't only surrounded by beautiful ingredients but I discovered a commitment to the pursuit of excellence. The ideas and memories laid out in the pages of this book derive from more than two decades I have spent at the stoves, each day striving to achieve higher standards, working with food and crafting the ultimate hedonistic product. I hope you will enjoy a glimpse into these memorable days and experiences.

If you don't feel like cooking, then stay away from the kitchen. Cooking is a labour of love. Some people say it's an art form, but I like to think of it as a craft. At my restaurant, we craft our food so that people can discover the love that has gone into it. At home it's the same thing, but it's even more intensified because you're cooking directly for the people closest to you – your friends, your family. To me, there's no better way to express that you care for them than by taking an ingredient and nurturing it, putting in a bit of this and a bit of that, and then watching them enjoy it. It's a great way of giving to the people you love. So if you're not in the mood, then get away from it, because you won't be able to cook with the kind of passion you need.

If you're in the kitchen with gusto, then even your failures will begin to taste good. I think failure in the kitchen is important because, just like in life, you can learn from your mistakes. Every failure is a step closer to success. Don't be intimidated by your tools or your ingredients; instead, respect and command them. Confidence is one of the key ingredients in successful cooking.

Make this book a kitchen-table book, not a coffee-table book. I encourage you to pick it up, read it and be inspired by it. I want you to take it into the kitchen and use it. Some of the ideas here have come from many years of experience and some have been improvised. They are all intended to inspire. This is a guide – a road map, if you like – but you can choose the direction in which to travel. The book is meant to take the shackles off home cooks, who sometimes feel they have to follow a formula or recipe rigidly to be able to cook something great. Take the methods used here, build on them, then enter the kitchen unchained and *create*.

Some of the recipes need to be adhered to more rigidly than others – pastry, say – but elsewhere you can use your own judgement. You already do this. When a recipe suggests a pinch of salt and your taste buds want more, you add more. Take gnocchi for example. People say, 'How many potatoes? How much flour?' Well, it depends on the size and type of the potatoes, and the amount of time you cook them for – if you cook them too much they'll be wetter and you'll need more flour, and that's bad because it will make the gnocchi harder. You need to put your hands in it and feel it. You really have to experience it a couple of times, because there are so many variables to the recipe that it may be different every single time you make it. The only way to get it consistent is to use your eye and your touch.

Get to know the ingredients. With experience, you'll find the essential knack of balancing ingredients and flavours. Cook with your fingers, your eyes and your heart rather than by following instructions (which is like painting by numbers), and you will express yourself through the food. Adding a bit of this and a bit of that along the way, you will create your own *cucina*.

I love to cook like this – some of my best work comes from being in the kitchen and feeling confident enough just to go for it. Some preparations can be very quick, with little effort needed, yet are very rewarding. Others require a certain length of time to do, and these preparations are part of the fundamentals, which need to be respected. Unchaining yourself in the kitchen doesn't necessarily mean not following any kind of system or procedure. There are certain things that need to be done properly so that you can achieve great depth of flavour. I like to use soup as an example of this because it has long been considered a restorative in many cuisines and at times is looked upon as having quasi-medicinal qualities. In a gastronomic sense, soups and broths have great depth of flavour. When you put a spoonful of beautiful soup in your mouth you can taste in the background the onions that have been fried and the vegetables that have been boiled gently and cooked for hours and hours, and every spoonful uncovers another layer. You can whack out a vegetable soup in 20 minutes, and it will be great, but I guarantee that if you cook it slower then the depth of flavour the salt extracts from the vegetables and other ingredients will really start to come to the fore on your palate.

Our ingredients provide us with both our greatest opportunities and our most difficult challenges. We must always seek out the very best. The objective is to treat a great ingredient with sensitivity – after all, it should still taste like the original ingredient when we are finished with it. Simplicity and freshness are the key factors, and buying produce seasonally makes good sense. Sure, these days with improved transport and more advanced methods of production, much produce is available all year round. But an ingredient is still generally at its best and cheapest during its optimum season. That's the time of the year it's most appropriately eaten. I admit it's a bit romantic, but I think it's comforting to bite into a prickly pear, or to enjoy the burst of flavour from a pomegranate seed, in late February. You know what month you're in. I love the change of seasons, saying goodbye to what we have been using in the kitchen and seeing the new produce appear on the market shelves to herald the new time of year. So where I have felt it appropriate in this book, I have added a note to a recipe, providing recommendations for the main ingredient's selection and use, and ideas on substitutions for it.

Cooking is influenced by environment: by people and their habits, by available produce and by climate. Today health awareness is also an important factor impacting on our food fashion. All of these things affect what we eat and how we eat it. Obviously, food styles have changed over the years. We've come full circle in a lot of ways. Things are becoming simpler again and people are looking for ingredients to be less adulterated and more pure, rather than trying to overly embellish them in cooking. I think that's a wonderful thing. We're going back to the market and looking for chickens that actually taste like chicken, rather than mass-produced things that have been treated poorly through their life and taste like absolutely nothing. And whereas once we said there was too much fat in our beef, now we're looking for beef that has good fat marbling in it, resulting in a rich flavour and a lovely, luscious tenderness when you bite into it. We are starting to find that even in our local shops there's a bit more care in the ingredients they're selling, so we're not just looking at an average, run-of-the-mill piece of meat. Instead, the shopkeeper knows where the meat has come from and how it's been grown, and the consumer is interested in that. Consumers in the family home drive such trends.

My cooking draws on traditional Italian fundamentals, but if there are ingredients that are more accessible here in Melbourne than in Italy, I don't turn my back on them just because they're not traditional. Italian cuisine has spread all over the world because it doesn't ignore local culture and produce. It adapts. This is not an Italian cookbook, but rather a Melbourne cookbook with an Italian heritage.

One person who shares my food philosophy is my brother-in-law and fellow chef, Chris Rodriguez. He and I have been working together for years developing what we consider our own style of Italian-Australian food.

I think Melbourne is a sophisticated city, but it's warm as well and has a lot of personality and character. Melburnians are passionate – there's always something they care about. Food happens to be one of the things I care about, but it may be theatre or the arts or footy for others. Footy's a fantastic example, because it's something where you can see raw passion, and Melburnians embrace it. Some of our restaurant's most sophisticated customers – they're well travelled, love their food and always want something to excite their palate – are diehard football supporters. I think that's the beauty of Melbourne. You can have a night at the ballet or the opera, or come to dinner at Grossi Florentino, or make sure you've got fresh oysters to shuck for the Sunday barbecue, but you can also get up on Saturday afternoon and scream your lungs out and carry on like a complete yahoo because your team's not doing as well as they should be doing.

I have some family in Milan – in Lombardia – a really big city where everything seems to happen. They've got the big fashion *sfilate*, and the massive Il Padiglione della Fiera di Milano, a pavilion where there are lots of international exhibitions. There's lots of people and it's very fast-moving, with lots of activity going on. If you made the city smaller, you'd have something very similar to Melbourne, where the people are just doing their thing, going about their business, but are quite sophisticated about what they're doing. That's how I feel about Melbourne. I reckon you can dine out on a different cuisine every night of the week for a month and still not hit the same one twice. It's unbelievable the selection we have. It's a really great town.

Food is an integral part of our everyday life, but obviously different occasions require different approaches to cooking. I have arbitrarily put the recipes in this book into sections that reflect certain occasions and cooking styles. For example, the chapter called 'Improvviso' deals with impromptu meals created directly from your pantry, 'Cool Food' presents great starter dishes that can be prepared ahead of time, and 'Loaves and Fishes' looks at simple and fun ways to create a feast for a big occasion. Naturally, the recipes are interchangeable for any event – it's up to you how you use them.

These Italian-themed pages are meant to inspire. Go into the kitchen and cook for someone you love. The pleasure will be mine.

Essentials

# The Cooking Room

The kitchen – the cooking room – is the hub of the household. Whether its design is sophisticated or simple, warmth and atmosphere are vital, because this is a workplace where inspiration is required.

If you're going to spend your time productively, then you need an environment that feels good. It must be clean – obsessively clean. I like a kitchen to have as little clutter as possible, allowing the cook to practise their craft freely, without encumbrance. I don't mind some tools being stored in view – this makes good sense if the utensils are used so regularly that it saves time and effort. My mortar and pestle, for example, sits in front of me all the time. I often need to crush or pound an ingredient quickly, and it would be silly to reach into a cupboard every time.

Good bench space is crucial, especially for preparing foods such as gnocchi or pasta, and for rolling out pastry. Clean, solid surfaces are preferable, with as few joins as possible and free of nooks and crannies. It's always handy to have a slab of marble if you can, and impervious surfaces on walls that can be washed down easily. A good, deep sink for washing up and washing food makes life a hell of a lot easier, too. I have a beautiful old gas stove with six burners and plenty of space, and two big ovens underneath. This set-up is fantastic. It gives me loads of room to have my pots simmering and a roast in the oven, and I can still be sautéing at the same time. I know it would be a luxury in many domestic kitchens, but it does make good sense to have a decent-sized stove, which also adds aesthetically to the cooking room.

# The Tools

Like every good craftsperson, a cook must have good tools. That doesn't necessarily mean the most expensive tools, but rather, practical equipment that is easily maintained. The most important thing is to have tools in the kitchen that are necessary, rather than ornamental. It's easy to get caught up with the latest bits and pieces, but you don't always need them. Some of the most useful equipment in the kitchen is the most basic. Here I list some of the things I always like to have on hand. You will have your own favourites to add.

**Knives:** As a minimum, I work with four knives and a cleaver: a cook's knife for chopping; a boning knife, essential for trimming meats; a filleting knife for fish; and a paring knife for smaller jobs. The cleaver I use for breaking bones. You do need a sharpening steel, because your knives must be sharp at all times – blunt knives are inefficient and dangerous. High-quality knives are not cheap, but I believe they're worth it. Your knives will get more use than any other equipment in the kitchen.

**Boards**: Go for impermeable boards that are easily cleaned. It's best to have more than one.

**Mortar and pestle:** I use a heavy stone mortar and pestle. It's great for making pesto and pounding dry ingredients like juniper berries and spices.

**Graters**: A very basic necessity. Having a couple of graters around the kitchen is better than having just one. A fine grater is needed for nutmeg and lemon zest.

**Grinders**: I always have a manual grinder handy that is loaded with black pepper, and I use a simple electric grinder for spices.

**Scales**: A set of electronic scales is an asset and saves a lot of headaches, especially if it can switch from metric to imperial measurements.

**Measuring jugs**: An assortment of metric jugs and cup measures in stainless steel is a great help.

**Spoons, scrapers, spatulas**: I like to have a range of stainless steel kitchen spoons, both slotted and solid, including ladles. Pastry scrapers and rubber spatulas are vital.

**Juicer**: I use a great little hand-held wooden juicer that gets right into the fruit.

**Wire racks**: These are essential for cooling breads and cakes.

**Colander**: How else would you be able to strain pasta and vegetables? Every well-equipped kitchen has one or two colanders.

**Mouli**: A decent-sized mouli, made of metal not plastic, is great use when making soup, and for tomatoes.

**Sieves (drum and fine)**: You need a drum sieve for passing foods of a more solid nature, such as ricotta. Some sauces require a fine strainer, which is also great for stocks.

**Potato ricer**: This is the best way to crush potatoes for gnocchi. They mash really well but stay fluffy.

**Blender, food processor**: I like to have a powerful blender for doing really fine purées and sauces, and a more robust food processor for heavier items.

**Whisks**: It's important to have a small range of whisks, varying in both size and weight.

**Mincer**: Having your own mincer is the best way of controlling the quality of your minced meats. It is also a great way of utilising offcuts and trimmings. A heavy hand-operated one will do the job.

**Thermometers**: A sugar thermometer is required for some recipes where the sugar has to be cooked at various stages above 100°C. A meat thermometer also comes in handy when roasting meat and cooking terrines.

**Pots, pans, roasting trays**: How can you have too many? Your budget and storage space will be your only restraints here. Choosing can be difficult when there is such a wide range available. I like heavier pots and pans. Good-quality stainless steel or copper ones retain heat really well and are an absolute pleasure to work with, but there are varying-quality aluminium ones that are more affordable. Iron or enamelled roasting trays are both excellent as long as they have the weight. A small range of good non-stick pans is a good idea for more delicate bits of food. I have a beautiful copper pot at home, in which I can seal all my ingredients first and then braise them – all in the one pot, *ottimo*. Make sure you have a sensible mix of sizes: larger pots for stocks and pasta, and smaller ones for sauces and the like.

**Storage trays and containers**: Needing to store something and having to scratch around for a container can be frustrating. Plastic containers with airtight lids are great, and they work in the freezer as well as the fridge. All food should be completely covered when being stored.

**Mixing bowls**: A sensible collection of stainless steel bowls is required for mixing ingredients. I like to use thick porcelain ones, too – they're so old fashioned.

**Pasta machine:** The type of machine you choose depends on how serious you want to get about your pasta. A small hand-operated machine will certainly do the trick. In any case, you must have one – it's extremely rewarding to make your own pasta.

**Tart cases, flan rings, cake tins**: An assortment is the key here. There are plenty to choose from, so have a good look around before you buy.

**Scissors**: Get a proper pair of kitchen scissors that will cut through fish and poultry easily.

**Pastry brushes, piping bags**: You will need a couple of good brushes, and a couple of piping bags with an assortment of nozzles.

# Buying Ingredients

A great dish starts with buying the food, and making sure you get good food. The basic rule to follow is: always choose high quality. You can make lousy food out of great ingredients, but you can't make great food out of lousy ingredients. It's impossible.

The first step in successful shopping is finding a good supplier. Supermarkets are much better than they once were, and they have an incredible range, but I'm a Melbourne boy through and through so I love shopping on the street, walking to my butcher and my grocer. It's also fantastic taking a walk around the Queen Victoria Market, which is world standard as far as atmosphere goes, and the variety is fabulous. There are beautiful meat and fish sections, and the Asian grocers are unbelievable.

A list is always a good thing to have before you go shopping, but you need to be open-minded and flexible with it. If your recipe calls for barramundi but the barramundi at the shop looks haggard and there's some perfectly good coral trout sitting next to it, then go for the trout – get the one that's best. Food is really like that. You have to be prepared to change things around so you can get the best of what's available right at that moment, when you're purchasing. That's why I love the inspirational variety at the Vic Market. It gives you great ideas – you might start with a dish of rabbit and leeks in mind, but end up deciding it's going to be rib-of-beef day, because of what you find. I think that's all part of the fun, being able to have that flexibility and enough confidence to change from your original plan.

Dealing with the people is just as important as the product. That is, being comfortable with your supplier and knowing them, so you can have the confidence to ask, 'Can you fix this for me?' or 'Could you clean that for me?' or 'Can you organise something else for me?' If you have that rapport, you get a lot more out of your supplier than if they don't know you from a bar of soap. If you've been in before and they know you're coming in again, they're usually a lot more helpful.

## Meat

There is lots of meat available that is pretty nondescript – it could be grown anywhere. Take beef, for example. The main thing I always look for is something quite large, and always out of ox, because ox is more flavoursome than cow meat. I always look for something with a decent amount of fat marbling, so there's enough moisture in the beef and it will cook well. At Grossi Florentino we've been buying wagyu beef, which is an expensive, specialist meat from the same strain of cattle as Japanese Kobe beef, but grown here in Australia. It's fantastic because of its richness and high fat content. It's lovely in flavour and luscious, and it cooks really well because there's good moisture in it.

We've also been buying pork that is quite fatty but really full of flavour, from a breed called black pig. This pork is getting away from commercially produced meats, which are all the same – really light in colour, not as fatty as pork used to be, and with a taste that can be insipid and ordinary. The thing I look for when buying pig, especially in larger cuts, is to buy the females. They taste nicer than the larger male pigs, which can be really smelly. If you roast a leg of pork and it smells really strong and has a horrible, musky flavour, it's because it's from a male pig that's grown too big. Female pigs taste a lot sweeter and more delicate. This doesn't matter so much with young suckling pigs, which are usually male because the sows are kept for breeding.

Suckling lambs also provide good meat. The beautiful Flinders Island suckling lambs we've been buying are grown very naturally. They're milk fed, still on their mothers, but have seen daylight. They've run around the paddock a bit, and are killed quite young, usually at 3–4 months. More mature lamb that has been reared by good growers can be delicious, too. Some recipes suit both the younger and more mature animal. Sourcing products like this is very exciting. You might think you'll never find them in your local butcher, but I believe that the driver of the end product is the consumer. If enough people go into a butcher shop and ask for such-and-such, the butcher will eventually start to source more decent products. It's up to the consumers to be interested enough to let the butcher know. Finding a good butcher and becoming friendly with them is really important if you want to acquire the best meat.

Game is becoming more widely available. The speciality stores at our main markets can usually access most kinds of game meat. Some, such as hare, still comes from the wild, but most of it is farmed to control quality. This is fine as long as care has been taken in its production.

Most veal we see these days is very young and does not have a great deal of flavour. Veal that is a little more developed, such as White Rocks veal from Western Australia, is delicious. At the White Rocks Dairy they grow their calves to 100 kg and feed them lots of milk, which results in meat with a wonderful rich pink colour and full flavour. The meat retains much of the characteristic tenderness associated with veal. Happily, other interesting brands of veal are now appearing on the market, too.

I love most kinds of offal, and have thus included some recipes that use it. The most crucial factor for achieving the best results is freshness, especially when dealing with such delicacies as kidneys, liver and giblets. Oxtail is one of my favourites; I like the flavour of a larger, more robust oxtail with good fat coverage. Tripe is not as commonly carried by butchers as it once was, so obtaining it may require more forethought than obtaining other kinds of offal. Brains (usually lamb's brains) can be purchased frozen, as can sweetbreads, but if you want to use the fresh items they can be obtained if you give your butcher a little warning.

Looking at some of the old Florentino menus, maybe from the 1930s, I've come across ones where the price of the chicken main course is more expensive than the lobster. At first I'd thought they were a mistake, but people who were around at the time have told me they're correct – chicken used to cost more than lobster and was more of a delicacy. I remember the days, even when we were kids, when you had a roast chicken at home as a very special, beautiful treat. I think we went through a sort of Dark Ages with chickens, when they were commercially produced in huge numbers in batteries. They were abused. These days there's a real swing back to getting chickens walking around and eating off the ground, giving them exercise and a decent life, and as a result they're starting to taste like chickens again. They're eating the right sort of feed to give their flesh flavour, and the colour of the meat is getting darker again, rather than being insipid white meat. The more expensive chickens in the shop are probably grown better.

The swing to try to get produce back to the way it was is happening across the board. As a society, we've started to realise there's been a price to pay for changing our production methods to satisfy economics. The food is cheaper to produce, but it's costing us in other ways. The animals are not having a great life because they're living terribly, and then once they're slaughtered, they don't have the same properties, flavour-wise, that they once had, because they're not as natural. This is why I'm also a firm believer that wild product is always better than farmed product. If the animals live in the wild, they do what they're naturally meant to do. Some of them have good lives, some of them have bad lives, but it's always a struggle for them to get through, and that generally makes them a better animal at the end of the day. Farmed barramundi is a classic example. The flesh of a farmed barramundi tends to be a lot more mushy, whereas that of a beautiful, wild barramundi tends to be quite firm. The wild fish are more active and are feeding themselves in the ocean. They're going into estuaries to breed and coming back out to the ocean. (Rabbits are an exception. I always like to buy farmed Victorian rabbits because of their consistency. With wild rabbits, the sizes are very similar no matter their age, and you could have an old boiler but not really know it.)

People are also more prepared now to sacrifice a bit of the tenderness in their meat if the flavour's right. You notice this in things like veal. We're getting more veal coming through that is perhaps grass fed, grown until it's a bit larger – and the flavour is getting better. Whereas once it might have been thought too chewy, these days it's more about flavour. I think food is about flavour, isn't it? At the end of the day, you want to put it in your mouth and you want it to have some sort of an impact or give you an experience. And that's where it's all going.

There are lots of butcher shops around Melbourne that do a decent job, such as Largo's in Brunswick. Good butchers run clean and helpful operations and are prepared to source high-quality products and accommodate special requests such as less-usual cuts and pre-orders of specialised products.

## Fish

You need a really good, reliable fishmonger that you trust, especially if you want them to cut and fillet the fish for you. We use Clamms Fast Fish in Acland Street, St Kilda, who have a beautiful range, always something fresh. There are many others – everyone will find their own favourite fishmonger. The shop should be clean and smell beautiful. Sometimes you walk into a fish shop and it smells *really* fishy. There's nothing wrong with this, but some fishy smells are terrible and some are really beautiful – sweet, fragrant, seafood sort of smells. And that's the sort of fish shop you want to walk into and buy fish from.

The notion of fish being fished out of the sea the night before you buy it is a fallacy. It doesn't happen that way. Fish moves around, coming directly from ships off the coast of Queensland or elsewhere, onto overnight freight, to the markets and fish shops. If all of this is a sound process and the fish is kept cold, it will have a shelf-life.

I always like to look at whole fish, because you can see how fresh it is from the head, gills and eyes. The eyes should be clear and protruding, and the flesh should be firm. If you press it, it should spring back slightly. Behind the gills is the first place where fish will start to smell, and smell is a very big indication for fish not being 100 per cent fresh.

## Fruit and vegetables

Greengrocers should have a good turnover. They should know their produce and seasonal varieties. For home, we use Toscano's in Kew. They always have a superb range, they're very professional, and

they sell a lot all the time, so you know that things are coming in and out of the place quickly.

If you're into seasonal produce, like I am, a greengrocer who enjoys keeping up with it is important. If your supplier just buys the basics, available all year round, then you won't be aware of when Jerusalem artichokes have come in again. I always get really excited about the appearance of asparagus, and I love seeing zucchini flowers come in, because that means summer has arrived. And pomegranates are only around for a minute – if you blink, you miss them – but they're great when fresh, with a beautiful burst of colour and flavour.

It's not necessarily true that the best-looking fruit and vegetables will taste best. I was once in a market in Italy where they were selling eggplant and fennel that looked a bit shabby, but when I cut into them they tasted magnificent. I couldn't figure out why they looked so shabby but tasted so great, until I understood that it was because they were so naturally grown. They were grown in the earth and not irrigated very well, so they had to struggle to get water out of the ground. They actually tasted like eggplant and fennel. Sometimes when you overwater things they come out looking really big and beautiful, but taste of water.

A good supplier will know who to buy from because they're in touch with their growers and they know some that are passionate about what they're doing and proud of their product.

# Herbs and Spices

I love herbs. They're such an integral part of cooking. With herbs, you can extract different flavours and give your cooking that lovely edge. There's nothing more beautiful than rosemary and lemon on roasting veal, and as soon as I start to pan-sauté calamari I want coriander. Or if I'm making a fish soup, I want to throw in some coriander, and a spice like cumin – not so that they overpower everything, but for that beautiful hint of fresh herb.

You can see whether herbs are fresh – they're beautiful and alive, and look like they've just been picked. If they've been sitting around on shelves for a bit too long, they look a bit weary and tired, and you're obviously not going to get the freshness and full benefit out of them. It's really nice if you can have a few herbs on hand in pots in the garden. You can't get fresher than that – snip some off, give it a wash and there you go. If you can afford the time and the luxury, it's handy to have a few pots around the garden, particularly with the resilient stuff like sage and rosemary, or even parsley, which tend to look after themselves quite well.

**Parsley**: In writing a list of the herbs I use most in my cooking, parsley has to be first. Fresh parsley is magnificent. It gives a lovely, just-cooked freshness, a suggestion of 'I've just finished off this dish'. I prefer continental or flat-leaf parsley for its flavour and aromatic qualities. It is a daily task in the Grossi Florentino restaurant kitchen to chop the parsley and it is always used up by the end of the day. Parsley is used throughout the Italian *cucina*. It has been known of at least since the time of the Romans, who used it to cover up the smell of alcohol on the breath after their notorious orgies, and also as an aid to digestion. Parsley is one of the easiest herbs to grow in your own garden as it regularly self-seeds, providing a constant crop.

**Rosemary**: Rosemary comes a close second to parsley in the amount I use in the kitchen, even though rosemary is more versatile. There are a number of regional Italian desserts that use it. It is a strong herb that needs to be used carefully, as it can easily overpower subtle flavours. Once I have stripped the leaves from a sprig, I put the woody stalk aside to use as a skewer to thread meat onto or to secure rolled meat. The flavour of the rosemary will then permeate the meat.

**Mint**: Like rosemary, this herb is used in all areas of cooking. It is associated more with desserts than with savoury dishes, but is a great flavour with vegetables and a surprising addition to soup. In Florentine cooking, catmint or nepitella is used more often than common mint; the Florentines love to make pesto from nepitella, just as others love to use basil.

**Basil**: Nothing says that summer is really here more than the slightly aniseed flavour and aroma of basil. Its beauty, like that of most herbs, lies in its adaptability. Basil enhances the flavour of many dishes. It has a superb oily quality in its leaves that gives it the ability to hold its flavour and colour when placed under oil. Pesto is made in huge quantities in our kitchen when basil is in season, so that I can use the wonderful flavour in my cooking long after summer is over.

**Coriander**: I know coriander is not particularly associated with the Italian kitchen, but I just love its flavour. It does have a past association with the Roman *cucina* – coriander was used in vinegar to preserve meats. The fresh, curly leaves are often mistaken for parsley when the plant grows large. Don't overlook the seeds when cooking, especially for heavier winter dishes.

**Myrtle**: Although it is not classified as a herb, myrtle is used in the kitchen in the manner of other herbs. I first experienced the flavour of the leaves in a suckling-pig dish in Rome. When I returned home I was surprised to find that we grow myrtle in Australia more as a garden bush than as a herb. I now have a number of myrtle plants in my garden that supply me for my own suckling-pig dishes. After the plant flowers, purple oval-shaped fruit follows. The Italians make a distilled liqueur called *mirto* by crushing the berries to extract the oil, in the same way as olive oil is made. In cooking, myrtle is used predominantly in Sardinia, where the plant grows alongside wild mint and thyme.

**Sage**: The wonderful flavour of sage is now known by many because of the ever-popular dish of *saltimbocca alla romana*. Sage is most commonly used in veal and chicken dishes, as its slightly musty flavour sits well with more delicate meats. Traditionally, it has been used more for medicinal purposes than for cooking. It was cited in a text used in the tenth century at the Salerno medical school, and was credited with increasing mental agility and longevity.

**Saffron**: Only a small amount of the golden powder of the Mediterranean is required to impart great depth of flavour – which is fortunate, as saffron is by far the most expensive product in the world to purchase by weight. The thin, dried, deep-orange stigma of the crocus flower releases an incredible amount of yellow colour when cooked. It is recognisable in many dishes, none more so than the *risotto milanese* traditionally served with osso buco.

**Star anise**: I love using star anise in duck and other game dishes, even if I add a sweet sauce of cherries or orange – all of these flavours work well together. The Romans realised the true value of anise and used it to pay taxes. They also made a cake laden with spices, in particular star anise, that was served at the end of a heavy meal or banquet to aid digestion. The cake became known as the 'wedding cake' because it was often served after a grand occasion.

**Bay leaves**: We have a large tree in the garden and I pluck the leaves fresh when I need them for my cooking. Bay is one of the few herbs that still retains much the same ability to impart flavour dried as fresh. Hang a cut branch upside down to allow the leaves to dry out. Once dried, pluck the leaves and put them into a sealed glass jar for use in soups, sauces and meat dishes. Do remember to remove bay leaves before serving, as they are unpleasant to bite into.

**Nutmeg**: Nutmeg has a most distinctive flavour and one that everyone, young and old, enjoys. I grate it fresh (using a grinder not dissimilar to a pepper grinder) into a surprising number of dishes, including *stracciatella*, a soup my mother believes cures all ills and made me eat a lot of when I was growing up. I also grind nutmeg into many casserole-style dishes, and of course it is used extensively in desserts and pastries. It is mostly sold as a ground powder but, like most spices, the flavour has a fresher quality when it is freshly ground, pounded or split. Investing in a metal-toothed nutmeg grinder is well worth it.

**Cinnamon**: The flavours of cinnamon and nutmeg could almost be considered an old married couple. One is usually not far from the other. For the most part cinnamon is used in its powdered form. If cinnamon sticks are used whole or in part, they must be removed before serving. When making dishes with milk that also require cinnamon, try heating the milk gently with the spice and then allowing it to cool. The flavour of the cinnamon will gently steep into the milk.

**Vanilla**: To most people over the past few decades, vanilla was known as a brown, almost black liquid that came in a bottle. How I love to see the real thing so readily available now, and that so many feel comfortable using vanilla pods! I add a pod to milk infusing with cinnamon and allow it to steep before using the liquid in desserts. The beauty of vanilla pods is that if they are treated right they can be used many times and still impart a great deal of flavour every time.

# Preparations

I have discussed with you the need for a well-organised work space, decent tools and excellent ingredients in order to be effective in the kitchen. Another important step is to have some basic and essential preparations on hand that are used in a wide variety of recipes. Care must be taken to ensure their quality, as they are the building blocks on which many recipes are founded. Following are the ones you will come across throughout the pages of this book.

## Salsa di pomodoro
TOMATO SAUCE

1 kg good-quality canned, peeled tomatoes *or* ripe tomatoes, peeled
120 ml olive oil
2 cloves garlic, finely chopped
1 large onion, finely chopped
120 g tomato paste
sea salt
freshly ground black pepper
1 cup water
4 basil leaves
½ cup freshly chopped oregano
30 g butter (optional)

Bring a large pot of water to the boil. If using fresh tomatoes, score the base of each with a sharp knife and put in the pot. Allow the water to return to the boil, then drain immediately. Wipe out the pot, add the olive oil and garlic and cook over a moderate heat. Add the onion and fry until it begins to colour. Stir in the tomato paste and cook for 2–3 minutes, stirring occasionally so it doesn't stick and burn. Add the tomatoes, season, and mix well. Pour in the water, bring to a boil and reduce the heat. Add the herbs and simmer gently for about 1 hour or until the sauce reduces to your required consistency and the tomatoes have all broken up. Pass the sauce through a food mill or strain through a fine sieve. Stir in the butter, if desired. *Makes 1 litre*

## Maionese
MAYONNAISE

3 egg yolks
1 teaspoon Dijon mustard
40 ml white-wine vinegar
900 ml olive oil
sea salt
freshly ground black pepper

Whisk the egg yolks, mustard and vinegar in a large bowl. Whisking constantly, slowly drizzle in the oil, at first drop by drop. The mixture will thicken and have a dull appearance. If it looks glossy, check to see that the oil is mixing in properly. To check if the mayonnaise has emulsified, dip a spoon in and look at the back of the spoon. If oil is floating on the top and the yolks have separated, add a little warm water to bring the mixture back together. Season with salt and pepper to taste. You should have a thick mixture in which a spoon will stand upright. If not, whisk in some more oil and adjust the flavour by adding a little more vinegar. *Makes 1 litre*

## Pesto di basilico
BASIL PESTO

100 g basil leaves
1 clove garlic
50 g pine nuts
50 g freshly grated Parmigiano-Reggiano
50 g freshly grated pecorino
sea salt
freshly ground black pepper
175 ml good-quality olive oil

Using a large mortar and pestle, crush together all the ingredients except the olive oil. Gradually blend in the olive oil to form an emulsified paste, adding only a small amount of oil to begin with, just to get the dry ingredients to move. As you work, continually scrape the mixture from the sides into the centre of the bowl. Store in the refrigerator for up to 2 weeks in a screwtop jar with a film of oil to cover. *Makes about 1½ cups*

1 kg beef bones
olive oil
1 onion, roughly chopped
    (including skin)
1 carrot, roughly chopped
1 stalk celery, roughly chopped
½ leek, roughly chopped
    and well washed
1 bay leaf
1 sprig thyme
handful of parsley stalks
4 black peppercorns
2 tablespoons tomato paste
200 ml red wine
4 litres cold water

## Brodo di manzo
BEEF STOCK

Preheat the oven to 200°C. Put the beef bones in a baking tray and bake for 30 minutes until browned all over. Meanwhile, heat a little olive oil in a large pot and fry the vegetables until slightly golden. Add the herbs and peppercorns and stir in the tomato paste. Cook for 2–3 minutes, then deglaze the pan with the red wine. Discarding any fat or liquid in the baking tray, put the bones into the pot and add the cold water. Bring to the boil, then reduce the heat and simmer for about 6 hours or until the stock has reduced by 25 per cent, removing any scum that rises to the surface. Remove from the heat and strain. Use the liquid as desired.
*Makes 2 litres*

Demi-glace: To turn the stock into demi-glace, reduce by half over a low heat. You will have a glossy, concentrated sauce.

1 kg veal bones
1 onion, roughly chopped
    (including skin)
½ carrot, roughly chopped
1 stalk celery, roughly chopped
½ leek, roughly chopped
    and well washed
olive oil
1 bay leaf
1 sprig thyme
handful of parsley stalks
4 black peppercorns
200 ml red wine
4 litres cold water
sea salt

## Brodo di vitello
VEAL STOCK

Preheat the oven to 200°C. Put the veal bones in a baking tray with the vegetables and a little olive oil and bake until browned all over. Remove from the oven, transfer the bones to a dish and set aside. Leaving any fat or liquid in the baking tray, put the vegetables, herbs and peppercorns into a large pot. Deglaze the tray with the wine and add to the pot. Pour in the water, add sea salt to taste and bring to the boil. Reduce the heat and simmer for about 4 hours, skimming off any oil or impurities that rise to the surface. Remove from the heat and taste, adjusting the seasoning if desired. Strain into a container and use as needed.
*Makes 3 litres*

## Brodo di pollo
CHICKEN STOCK

1 kg chicken bones
1 onion, roughly chopped
1 carrot, roughly chopped
1 stalk celery, roughly chopped
½ leek, roughly chopped and well washed
1 bay leaf
1 sprig thyme
handful of parsley stalks
4 black peppercorns
1 teaspoon sea salt
4 litres cold water

Wash the chicken bones well, then drain and put into a large pot with the remaining ingredients. Heat gently over a low heat until simmering, skimming the surface of any impurities. Simmer for about 3 hours, taking care not to let it boil rapidly, as this will make the stock go cloudy. Remove the pot from the heat and taste; the stock should have a distinct flavour of chicken. Gently strain the stock into a container and use as needed. *Makes 3 litres*

## Brodo di pesce
FISH STOCK

1 kg fish bones
2 teaspoons butter
1 small onion, roughly chopped
1 bay leaf
1 tablespoon freshly chopped dill
1 tablespoon freshly chopped coriander
handful of parsley stalks
4 black peppercorns
1 stalk celery, roughly chopped
½ leek, roughly chopped
    and well washed
200 ml white wine
4 litres cold water
1 tablespoon sea salt

Rinse the fish bones under cold running water to remove all blood and impurities. Chop roughly with a large knife, making sure to sever any spines. Melt the butter in a large pot and fry the onion until slightly soft. Add the fish bones, herbs and peppercorns and fry until the onion is fully soft. Add the celery and leek, then deglaze with the wine. Pour in the water, add the salt and simmer for 20–30 minutes. Remove from the heat and taste, adjusting the seasoning if desired. Strain into a container and use as needed. *Makes 3 litres*

## Brodo di verdura
VEGETABLE STOCK

2 onions, roughly chopped
1 carrot, roughly chopped
2 stalks celery, roughly chopped
1 leek, roughly chopped
    and well washed
1 turnip, peeled and roughly chopped
2 cloves garlic, peeled and roughly chopped
2 bay leaves
½ cup freshly chopped flat-leaf parsley
1 chilli, seeded and roughly chopped
    (optional)
3 litres cold water
sea salt
freshly ground black pepper

Put the vegetables, herbs and chilli (if using) in a large pot and cover generously with the water. Season with salt and pepper. Heat gently until simmering, skimming the surface of any impurities. Simmer for at least 1 hour until the stock is flavoursome. Gently strain into a container and use as needed. *Makes 2 litres*

## Pasta fresca
FRESH PASTA DOUGH

Sift the flours and salt into the bowl of an electric mixer fitted with a dough hook. Add the eggs one at a time and knead on low speed for about 10 minutes. Add a little water, if required – the dough should be soft but not sticky. Divide the dough into 2–3 pieces so it is easier to work with. Roll out each piece by pushing it through a pasta machine on the highest setting. Fold it in half and run through the machine again several times, folding each time. (If you do not have a pasta machine, use a rolling pin on a floured surface.) This process is called laminating. You need to laminate the pasta until it looks and feels silky smooth, like a baby's bottom. Adjust the setting on the pasta machine each time and roll the pasta until it is 1–2 mm thick. Cut into your desired shapes for filling, or into long strips, such as for tagliarini, fettuccine, pappardelle etc. (If you do not have a pasta machine, roll up the sheet of dough and cut through it with a very sharp knife to make long pasta such as tagliarini.) Spread out the pasta on a floured tray and cook on the same day as you make it.   *Makes 1.25 kg*

500 g unbleached flour
500 g durum-wheat flour
pinch of salt
8 eggs

## La pizza
PIZZA DOUGH

Put the water, oil, yeast and salt into the bowl of an electric mixer fitted with a dough hook. Knead on low speed until the yeast has dissolved. Add the flour and continue to knead for about 15 minutes until the dough is shiny and elastic. Cover the bowl with a clean tea towel and rest it in a warm area for 30 minutes–1 hour until doubled in size. Use the dough as desired.   *Makes 1 × 40 cm pizza or 2 × 24 cm pizzas*

1 cup lukewarm water
1 tablespoon olive oil
20 g fresh yeast
small pinch of salt
2 cups unbleached flour

To make a pizza: Lightly but thoroughly oil a pizza tray. Flour your work surface and tip the dough onto it. Using your hands, work the dough into a smooth ball, bringing the sides in towards the bottom. Put it onto the pizza tray and cover with a clean tea towel, then allow to prove for 15 minutes (the dough should grow again as it proves). Press the ball of dough down, stretching it to cover the tray. It should be no more than 1 cm thick. Top with your chosen ingredients and bake for 12–15 minutes in a hot oven (200°C) or until the bottom is golden brown.

## Biga
### STARTER BREAD DOUGH

¼ teaspoon instant dried yeast
½ cup warm water
3½ cups unbleached strong flour
1 tablespoon salt
1¼ cups water

Dissolve the yeast in the warm water and set aside until it froths. Combine the flour and salt in a large bowl and form a well in the centre. Pour in the yeast mixture and water and, using a wooden spoon, mix well. The dough should be sticky and hard to stir. Cover and refrigerate for 24 hours until ready to use. If not using immediately, divide into 4–5 pieces and freeze.   *Makes 1 kg*

## Pasta sfoglia
### PUFF PASTRY

500 g flour
1 teaspoon salt
300 ml cold water
400 g butter, cold but pliable

Sift the flour and salt together onto your workbench and make a well in the centre. Add the water gradually into the centre and hand mix to make a paste. Knead until the dough is smooth and elastic, then form into a ball, cover with plastic wrap and leave to rest for 30 minutes. Sprinkle some flour on your workbench and roll out the dough evenly to form a 20 cm square. Put the butter in the centre of the square and fold over the dough to enclose it completely, making a square block shape. Refrigerate for 10 minutes. Roll out the pastry to form a 30 cm × 10 cm sheet about 1.5 cm thick. Fold the sheet into three and roll out again to the same size. Repeat the folding and rolling, then refrigerate for 10 minutes. Repeat this process until the pastry has been turned 6 times in total, each time folding it in a different direction to the last time. Refrigerate for at least 20 minutes before use. Cut off your required quantity of dough and roll out on a floured surface to a thickness of 1 cm. Cut to your desired shape with a sharp knife or cutter and put on a floured tray. To cook, bake at 180°C for 12–15 minutes, or proceed according to recipe. Any leftover dough can be wrapped in plastic wrap and frozen until required. Defrost it in the refrigerator overnight.   *Makes 1 kg*

Notes
- To obtain perfect puff pastry, the dough and the butter must be of the same consistency – cold but pliable.
- The butter must not be too rigid when it is put inside the dough.
- The pastry must be kept cold while resting, but not chilled for too long. Excessive cold will cause the butter to harden and crack the pastry.
- Each time the pastry is rolled out, it must be in a regular shape, i.e. keep the sides and ends parallel to each other and the thickness even.

## Pasta frolla
SHORTCRUST PASTRY

Put the flour and salt in a large bowl and rub in the butter until the mixture has a sandy texture. Add the water a little at a time and mix until you have a large, smooth ball. Knead for about 5 minutes, then wrap in plastic wrap and refrigerate for 30 minutes. Roll out to your required thickness and line your tart case, using the rolling pin to ease the pastry over the case. Push the dough into place with your fingers and trim the edges. To blind bake, preheat the oven to 160°C. Line the pastry with foil and fill with dried beans or uncooked rice. Put the tart case on an oven tray and bake for 12–15 minutes if large, or 10–12 minutes for small tart cases. Allow to cool, then proceed according to recipe. *Makes 1.5 kg*

1 kg flour
1 tablespoon salt
500 g softened butter
200 ml water

## La polenta
POLENTA

Salt the water and bring it to the boil in a large pot. Add the polenta in a steady stream, stirring constantly. When all of the polenta has been added, stir for 2–3 minutes, then reduce the heat and simmer for 15–20 minutes, stirring occasionally. Stir in the Parmigiano-Reggiano and butter and season to taste with salt and pepper. Serve immediately. *Serves 6–10*

salt
2 litres water
500 g polenta
200 g freshly grated Parmigiano-Reggiano
20 g butter
freshly ground black pepper

## Sciroppo
SUGAR SYRUP

Put the sugar and water in a heavy-based saucepan and stir until the sugar has dissolved. Bring to the boil over a high heat and boil for 15 minutes. Remove from the heat and allow to cool. Store in a sealed container. The syrup keeps well for up to 1 week. *Makes 1.5 litres*

1 kg caster sugar
1 litre water

## Crema pasticcera
PASTRY CREAM

8 egg yolks
250 g caster sugar
100 g flour
1 litre milk
1 vanilla bean

Whisk the egg yolks and sugar in a stainless steel bowl for 5 minutes until creamy. Add the flour and a little of the milk and blend until smooth. Heat the remaining milk in a saucepan, with the vanilla bean, to just before boiling point. Remove the vanilla bean, then slowly whisk the hot milk into the egg mixture. Return to the saucepan and whisk until thick. Allow the mixture to cook gently for 2 minutes before removing from the stove. Cool. The pastry cream will keep for 3–4 days in the refrigerator, covered.   *Makes about 1.2 litres*

## Crema di mandorle
FRANGIPANE

60 g unsalted butter
60 g caster sugar
60 g almond meal
1 egg
1 heaped tablespoon flour

Cream the butter and sugar, then add the almond meal and whisk until well combined. Add the egg and flour and whisk again until well combined.   *Makes about 200 g*

Cool Food

The cold section of the menu has always intrigued me. It's a place where you can be really creative, where you're not restricted by cooking times. You can prepare ahead, and delve into things like beautiful marinades and pickles. It's a lovely area to experiment with different flavours and produce.

Working in the cold section also opens the cook to a world of colour. The variety of hues you can have on the plate is akin to an artist working on a canvas, except that you can eat your spoils when your work is done!

The cold larder emphasises the freshness and quality of produce. There's no masking of flavours, no disguise – so you can straight away detect any fault in the quality of the ingredients. Cool food absolutely depends on the best ingredients you can find.

It's no wonder I have such a love for the cold section of the menu, because it's where I began my professional cooking career. As a young apprentice, the world of the professional kitchen, with the staff in starched white jackets and tall hats, filled me with awe and respect for the knowledge these people had and that I was about to share. I looked forward to coming to work on a cold morning and going into the warmth of the kitchen, where the heat from baking bread enveloped me. Alas, the warm feeling was short-lived – it was my job to wash lettuces and open oysters, and my fingers would often be as cold as the produce I was preparing.

Despite this, working in the larder gave me the opportunity to work with produce selected because it was at its premium and was to be served without altering its natural splendour. I learnt that olive oils could vary in their flavour as well as their colour, and that even different salts could taste different. I was also surprised to discover unusual combinations of flavours that I never would have believed to be enjoyable.

Food that doesn't need any reheating is, of course, great for picnicking. As long as it's beautiful and fresh, with all the cooking and preparation done, there's no need for anything except opening the lid and helping yourself.

Enjoy your cold larder. It can be a very creative section of the kitchen, where you can show a lot of initiative and cover a range of cooking techniques. You need to hone a few skills to master these, but it's worth it.

# Antipasto

The word antipasto translates as 'before the meal'. In an Italian sense, it's the teaser, getting the party started so that – heaven forbid! – your guests are not sitting around without food. At an Italian meal, there is generally a little antipasto on the table, whether it be a simple nibble or a more elaborate spread of preserved vegetables, pickled fish or beautiful cured meats.

I think antipasto typifies that whole Italian family feel of bringing people to the table and sharing. In the restaurant we offer *grissini* and olives, so as people walk in there's some hospitality there, some warmth while they're settling in. There's nothing like breaking the ice with a bit of food on the table. It helps to get things moving along, because you can't just sit there, you need to participate – to reach over and help yourself to an olive, or ask someone to pass you an olive, or offer one to someone else. So *antipasti* have a psychological place at the dinner table, as well as a nutritional one.

The variety of antipasto is endless. What each cook chooses to make is very individual. You can serve so many things, from mushrooms to soused fish to lovely prosciutto or delicious salami. There's nothing nicer than picking at a bowl of freshly roasted peppers that have been laid out with a bit of garlic and some basil leaves – they're just so sweet and delicious.

The recipes in this section are designed to be part of an antipasto spread. Several of them keep really well and can be made a few days in advance. Some will feed more than others, but as a general rule each recipe will serve 4 people as a nibble or 2 people as an entrée.

*Smoked swordfish has a delicate flavour and a silky texture. This terrine makes great use of the product, adding a few other elements that do not steal its thunder.*

# Terrina di pesce spada

## SWORDFISH TERRINE

Brush a char-grill pan with a little oil and lightly grill the eggplant on both sides. Drain on kitchen paper and allow to cool. Chop the anchovies to a paste. Using an electric mixer, whip the butter until creamy, then add the anchovy paste and whip until smooth.

Lightly oil a terrine mould, then line the bottom and sides with plastic wrap, leaving some hanging outside the mould ready to be folded over the finished terrine. Line the mould with eggplant slices, overlapping them at the bottom and leaving enough hanging out to fold over the top of the terrine once the mould has been filled. Spoon a thin layer of anchovy butter into the bottom of the terrine dish, then top with a thin layer of smoked swordfish. Continue to layer the butter and swordfish until the mould is half-full. Sprinkle with the dill, then continue layering the butter and swordfish almost to the top of the mould, finishing with a layer of butter. Cover with eggplant slices. Fold overlapping plastic wrap over the terrine to seal well. Place a light weight on top and refrigerate overnight.

When ready to serve, unwrap the terrine and carefully invert it onto a board. Lift off the mould and remove the plastic wrap. Using a very sharp knife, cut the terrine into 1 cm slices.

Note: Good delicatessens will be able to help you source smoked fish. We buy ours from Tom Cooper, but there are other producers around the country. If you can't find smoked swordfish, smoked salmon is a good substitute.

olive oil
1 medium eggplant, thinly sliced
4 anchovy fillets
100 g softened butter
400 g smoked swordfish (*see* Note), thinly sliced
1 tablespoon freshly chopped dill leaves

*I created this dressing to serve with oysters. I wanted something with a bit of acid to cut the creaminess of the shellfish, but wasn't too tart. The verjuice really works well and the apple gives a burst of sweetness.*

# Agresto con mele

## APPLE AND VERJUICE DRESSING

1 Granny Smith apple, peeled and diced
1½ cups verjuice
1 teaspoon freshly chopped rosemary
1½ tablespoons olive oil
sea salt
freshly ground black pepper

Put the apple, verjuice and rosemary into a pot and cook over a medium heat for about 10 minutes, stirring occasionally, until the apple is tender. Stir in the olive oil and season to taste with salt and pepper, then remove from the heat and allow to cool. Serve with your favourite type of oysters. The dressing will keep for 1–2 days stored in an airtight container in the refrigerator.   *Makes 2 cups*

*Such an old-fashioned simple start to a meal, this one is always a favourite. My family love these eggs and there's always a race to get one before they all go.*

# Uova tonnate

## TUNA-FILLED EGGS

6 eggs
1 × 100 g tin good-quality tuna in oil (*see* Note), drained
3 tablespoons Mayonnaise (see page 18)
sea salt
freshly ground black pepper

Boil the eggs for about 7 minutes, then refresh in cold water and allow to cool. Shell the eggs and cut in half lengthways. Remove the yolks and set aside. Arrange the whites on a serving dish. Using an electric blender, quickly combine the tuna, egg yolks and mayonnaise to form a paste, then season with salt and pepper. Spoon into the egg whites and serve.

Note: Preserved (tinned) tuna ranges in quality dramatically. I always use good-quality Italian or Spanish tuna, either in olive oil or in brine depending on the recipe. Tuna in brine is lighter in taste (and kilojoules) but the texture can be drier.

*Opposite: Native flat oysters (Ostrea angasi) with Agresto con Mele, served with a bloody mary cocktail*

*This southern Italian preparation is one of the tastiest ways to eat mussels.*

# Cozze gratinate

## MUSSELS AU GRATIN

12 large mussels in the shell, cleaned
1 cup dried breadcrumbs
½ cup freshly grated Parmigiano-Reggiano
1 fresh red chilli, seeded and chopped
1 clove garlic, finely chopped
2 tablespoons freshly chopped flat-leaf parsley
¼ cup olive oil
grated zest of 1 lemon
sea salt
freshly ground black pepper

Preheat the oven to 180°C. Using a small butter knife (not a sharp knife), open each mussel by inserting the knife between the shells and prying them open. Remove all of the flesh from the top shell and transfer to the intact lower shell. Discard the empty top shells and arrange the lower shells on a baking tray. Mix the remaining ingredients except the salt and pepper, then season to taste. Spoon a little mixture onto each mussel, enough just to cover the flesh. Bake for 10 minutes until golden. Serve hot or at room temperature.

*The preparation works well with most fish and can be used for poultry as well. The sweetness of the onion provides a soft contrast to the vinegar.*

# Pesce in scapece

## SOUSED FISH

500 g white fish fillets (such as blue eye)
flour
500 ml cottonseed *or* vegetable oil
100 ml olive oil
2 onions, finely sliced
1 clove garlic, finely chopped
2 cloves
2 bay leaves
pinch of saffron threads
sea salt
freshly ground black pepper
1 cup white-wine vinegar
1 cup white wine
1 litre water

Cut the fish across into 2 cm strips. Dust with flour and pat with your fingers to remove any excess. Heat the cottonseed oil in a heavy-based pan and fry the fish in batches until golden brown. Drain on kitchen paper.

In a large, heavy-based saucepan, heat the olive oil and sauté the onion and garlic until soft and translucent and only slightly coloured. Add the remaining ingredients and bring to the boil. Reduce the heat and simmer gently, uncovered, for 20 minutes or until the onions are well cooked. Remove from the heat and allow to cool to room temperature.

Arrange the fried fish pieces on a flat dish and pour over the cooled dressing. Allow to stand for at least 1 hour before serving.

Note: The word *scapece* refers to a method of preserving food in vinegar, sweet-and-sour style. It is known as *carpione* in northern Italy and *saor* in Venice.

*Opposite: Cozze Gratinate*

*There was always a prickly pear plant in the backyard when I was growing up as it was a favourite fruit of my dad's. My brother and sisters and I would pick them and have prickly fingers for days.*

## Bresaola con fico d'India

### BRESAOLA WITH PRICKLY PEAR

16 slices bresaola (*see* Note)
4 prickly pears
freshly shaved Parmigiano-Reggiano
sea salt
freshly ground black pepper
extra-virgin olive oil

Arrange the *bresaola* on a serving dish. Using gloves, remove and discard the skin from the prickly pears. Thinly slice the prickly pears and scatter the slices over the *bresaola*. Garnish with Parmigiano-Reggiano and grind on a little salt and pepper. Drizzle with oil and serve.

Note: *Bresaola* is air-dried beef. It is a Lombardian speciality and has become more common in Australia in recent years. In flavour it is more delicate than prosciutto and not as salty.

*Years ago at the restaurant my fellow chef Chris and I had some cold fried calamari left over one night. We put some oil and vinegar and herbs on it and had it for supper. With each mouthful our tastebuds went nuts – we knew we were onto something.*

## Insalata di calamari

### FRIED CALAMARI SALAD

1 kg calamari, cleaned
flour
1 litre olive oil
1 bulb fennel, finely sliced
2 handfuls mâche
    (lamb's lettuce), washed
extra-virgin olive oil

*Dressing*
2 cups extra-virgin olive oil
200 ml white-wine vinegar
1 clove garlic, finely chopped
1 fresh chilli, seeded and
    finely chopped
¼ cup finely chopped
    coriander leaves
1 cup freshly chopped
    flat-leaf parsley
juice of 1 lemon
sea salt
freshly ground black pepper

Cut the calamari bodies into 3–4 cm × 1 cm strips, and the tentacles into bunches 6 cm long, then dust with flour and shake off the excess. Deep-fry the calamari in batches in hot olive oil for about 3 minutes until golden brown. Lift from the oil with a slotted spoon and drain on kitchen paper.

Mix all the dressing ingredients, seasoning with salt and pepper to taste. Gently toss the fried calamari in the dressing, then divide among serving plates. Lightly toss the fennel and mâche with a little extra-virgin olive oil. Garnish the calamari with the green salad and serve.

*Opposite: Fichi d'India*

*Here is an easy way of preparing your own cured meat. The back leg of the pig is my preferred cut for this dish because it has the richness needed.*

# Maiale salmistrato

## PICKLED PORK

1 kg pork loin, skin on
leaves from 2 handfuls flat-leaf parsley
2 tablespoons Dijon mustard
1 teaspoon freshly cracked black pepper
2 bay leaves
water
200 g freshly shaved pecorino

*Dressing*
200 ml olive oil
100 ml white-wine vinegar
1 teaspoon Dijon mustard
pinch of sea salt
pinch of freshly ground black pepper

Using a sharp knife, make numerous small cuts in the meat. Stuff the cuts with parsley, pushing it deep into each crevice. Spread the mustard over the meat and sprinkle with the cracked pepper. Lay out a large sheet of plastic wrap on your work surface. Put the seasoned pork on it and lay the bay leaves on top. Wrap the meat tightly in the plastic wrap, then wrap in aluminium foil and tie securely with string. Put the wrapped pork into a deep, heavy-based pot and cover with water. Bring to the boil, then reduce the heat to a gentle simmer and cook for 1 hour. Turn off the heat and allow the meat to cool in the water. Remove from the water and refrigerate overnight.

To make the dressing, combine all ingredients.

Untie the string and unwrap the pork. Slice the meat thinly and serve with shavings of pecorino, drizzled with the dressing and scattered with extra parsley leaves if desired.

*I like to use pickled tongue here. Fresh tongue works, but the flavour will differ.*

# Lingua di bue in salsa verde

## OX TONGUE WITH SALSA VERDE

1 ox tongue
½ onion, sliced
2 bay leaves

*Salsa verde*
2 cups olive oil
2 cups white vinegar
leaves from 2 handfuls flat-leaf parsley
1 stick celery, chopped
½ clove garlic
1 slice stale white bread, crusts removed
1 tablespoon capers
½ small chilli
sea salt
freshly ground black pepper

Rinse the tongue well, then put it into a large saucepan and cover with water. Add the onion and bay leaves. Bring to the boil, then reduce the heat and simmer very gently for 1 hour. Remove the tongue from the cooking liquid and set aside until it is cool enough to handle.

Using a sharp knife, peel off the skin from the tongue and trim off any excess fat. Slice the tongue thinly and arrange on a serving plate.

To make the salsa verde, put all the ingredients into an electric blender and blend until well combined. Strain through a fine sieve. Gently pour all of the sauce over the tongue. Leave for at least 30 minutes (or up to 24 hours) before serving.

*Opposite:* Maiale Salmistrato

# Cool First Courses

Cool dishes are a great prelude to a meal because they really get the tastebuds going and have you wanting more. A chilled stuffed fish or a rabbit terrine can make a magnificent presentation, and if you've got a few other bits and pieces it can be built up into an entire meal. The greatest thing is that you can do a lot of this stuff ahead of time. It can be laid out and ready to go for when somebody turns up.

People often have a misconception that with cold food there's not much cooking, but there can be a lot. You can buy an oyster, shuck it and squeeze a piece of lemon on it, and there's no cooking. You can't beat this – it's natural, fresh and beautiful, and very, very simple. But if you're doing something like a stuffed fish, there's a bit more involved. You might stuff it with scallops, wrap it in leeks and poach it in the oven in fish stock, then take it out and chill it so it can be sliced and served. It's a cold dish, but there's cooking involved.

While antipasto dishes lend themselves to an environment where everyone can help themselves, these cool first courses are plated entrées. They are great in hot weather, but might also be dishes that simply work really well served cold. For example, the roasted porcini and eggplant (see page 45) is dressed and served as a cold cish, but is great in cool weather too because the flavours are rich and sumptuous. The octopus terrine (page 43) works well in hot weather and the fish *carpaccio* (page 39) is another lovely cold entrée. Most of the dishes in this section can be built up to be a main-course meal by increasing the quantities of ingredients.

*I had this lovely entrée for the first time in Rome many years ago, in a beautiful seafood restaurant. It was a white fish, probably like a blue eye cod or similar, which had been sliced very thinly and marinated in blood orange juice, freshly cracked pepper and beautiful herbs. The acid in the citrus lightly cooks ('cures') the fish.*

500 g white fish (*see* Note)
100 ml blood orange *or* other citrus juice
100 ml extra-virgin olive oil
1 teaspoon capers
1 tablespoon freshly chopped flat-leaf parsley
1 teaspoon freshly chopped dill leaves
2 pinches grated lemon zest
sea salt
freshly ground black pepper
baby silverbeet leaves (optional)

# Carpaccio di pesce bianco

WHITE FISH CARPACCIO WITH CITRUS

Using a sharp knife, slice the fish very thinly. Arrange the fish on a serving platter.
 Combine the citrus juice, olive oil, capers, herbs and lemon zest, then pour over the fish. Season to taste with salt and pepper. Allow to marinate for at least 30 minutes. Serve garnished with baby silverbeet leaves, if using.   *Serves 4*

Note: As this fish is served raw, it is absolutely vital that you select only the freshest and highest quality available. I like to use a firm-fleshed fish such as swordfish or blue eye, or perhaps coral trout. Spanish mackerel will also work, but because of its oilier flesh it will give a richer result.

*Sweet, delicate crab is a special treat as it is relatively expensive to purchase. This simple way of serving it has all the good things a crab needs — some chilli for spice, pomegranate for sweetness and cucumber for a fresh finish. The salmon roe also gives a burst of freshness.*

2 slices day-old bread, crusts removed
400 g freshly picked crab meat
   (see Note)
sea salt
freshly ground black pepper
½ small chilli, seeded and diced
¼ red onion, finely sliced
1 tomato, peeled, seeded and cubed
1 teaspoon freshly chopped
   flat-leaf parsley
1 teaspoon freshly chopped
   coriander leaves
1 stick celery,
   cut into thin 4 cm batons
4 tablespoons Mayonnaise
   (see page 18)
1 large cucumber, thinly sliced
   lengthways
1 tablespoon salmon roe (see Note)
handful of baby coriander leaves
   (optional)

*Pomegranate salmoriglio*
1 pomegranate, halved
1 cup extra-virgin olive oil
sea salt
freshly ground black pepper
2 teaspoons vincotto
   (or to taste; see Note)

# Insalata di granchio

## CRAB SALAD WITH POMEGRANATE SALMORIGLIO

To make the pomegranate *salmoriglio*, hold half a pomegranate over a bowl and tap the skin with a spoon until most of the seeds have dropped into the bowl. Remove any remaining seeds with the spoon and add to the bowl. Repeat with the other pomegranate half. Mix the pomegranate seeds and olive oil in a small bowl. Season with salt and pepper, then add the *vincotto* and mix well.

Preheat the oven to 180°C or the griller to moderate. Cut the bread into 1 cm cubes and spread on a baking tray. Toast in the oven or under the griller for a few minutes until golden. Allow to cool.

Put the crab meat in a bowl and season to taste with salt and pepper. Mix in the chilli, onion, tomato and parsley, then add the coriander, celery and mayonnaise and combine gently. Gently toss through the croutons.

Arrange the sliced cucumber in a circle on each plate to form a cup. Fill with the crab mixture and drizzle with the *salmoriglio*. Garnish with the salmon roe and baby coriander leaves (if using) to serve.   *Serves 4*

Note: My favourite crab variety is mud crab but I love blue swimmer as well. See what is available and then make up your own mind. Salmon roe is available from your fishmonger; I like the Yarra Valley brand. *Vincotto* is a syrupy liquid made by cooking grape must (the unfermented juice from pressing grapes). It is a speciality of Puglia, my father's native region, and has been well embraced in Australia even though it is relatively new to local cooks. *Vincotto* is used in dressings and sauces, both sweet and savoury. It is available from specialist food stores.

# Terrina di polipo con crostini di pomodoro

## OCTOPUS TERRINE WITH TOMATO CROSTINI

½ cup olive oil
1 onion, roughly chopped
1 stick celery, roughly chopped
1 kg fresh octopus tentacles (see Note), washed and well drained
water
juice of 2 lemons
sea salt
freshly ground black pepper
1 clove garlic, chopped
1 fresh chilli, seeded and chopped
1 tablespoon freshly torn *or* crushed basil leaves
1 tablespoon freshly chopped flat-leaf parsley
6 gelatine leaves (10 g in total)

*Tomato crostini*
50 g butter
2 tomatoes, peeled, seeded and chopped
½ clove garlic, finely chopped
1 teaspoon freshly chopped tarragon
8 slices baguette

Heat the oil in a deep, heavy-based pot. Add the onion and celery and sauté for 2–3 minutes, then add the octopus and stir for 2–3 minutes. Pour in water to cover the octopus. Add half the lemon juice and season with salt and pepper. Bring to the boil, then reduce the heat and simmer for 30 minutes or until tender when pressed with the fingers. (A larger octopus may take longer.) Transfer the octopus to a bowl, then set aside until it is cool enough to handle. Strain and reserve the cooking liquid.

Using your fingers, remove and discard the membranes from the octopus. Transfer to a clean bowl. Season with salt and pepper and dress with some of the reserved cooking liquid. Stir in the garlic, chilli, basil and parsley and add the remaining lemon juice to taste. Put 2 cups of the reserved cooking liquid into a small saucepan and heat. Soak the gelatine leaves in water for 1–2 minutes, then squeeze and stir into the hot cooking liquid until dissolved. Set aside.

Lightly oil a terrine mould, then line the bottom and sides with plastic wrap, leaving some hanging outside the mould ready to be folded over the finished terrine. Arrange the octopus tentacles lengthways in the mould in layers until the mould is almost full, making sure that the flavours and aromatics that have dressed the tentacles are also included. Pour in the liquid containing the gelatine. Fold the overlapping plastic wrap over the terrine to seal well. Place a light weight on top and refrigerate overnight.

Just before serving the terrine, make the tomato crostini. Melt the butter in a saucepan, then add the tomato, garlic and tarragon and cook gently for about 10 minutes or until the tomato is completely soft. Meanwhile, toast the baguette slices until golden. Top each baguette slice with a spoonful of cooked tomato and divide among serving plates.

Unwrap the top of the terrine and carefully invert it onto a board. Lift off the mould and remove the plastic wrap. Using a very sharp knife, cut the terrine into 1 cm slices. Arrange the terrine slices beside the crostini. Sprinkle the terrine with sea salt, if desired, and serve.

Note: Fresh baby octopus, which are about the size of a clenched fist, are generally of a high quality, but for this terrine it is better to use larger, more mature octopus. (The golfball-sized frozen product referred to as a 'baby octopus' is of very poor quality – do not use this.)

*Some people have a fascination with buffalo-milk mozzarella – I watch them at the dining table picking slices out of the salad and leaving none for those with more placid natures. I remember the first time I tried real Italian buffalo mozzarella, I was in Italy – the only place you could get it in those days – and a plate was put in front of me with a large, thick, oozing slice of the white cheese. I took a taste and was excited and delighted by its full flavour.*

# Melanzane con porcini, asparagi e mozzarella di bufalo

## ROASTED EGGPLANT WITH PORCINI, ASPARAGUS AND BUFFALO-MILK MOZZARELLA

2 medium eggplants
sea salt
8 large spears asparagus, peeled
100 g dried porcini mushrooms (*see* Note), soaked overnight
olive oil
1 clove garlic, finely chopped
1 teaspoon freshly chopped sage
1 tablespoon freshly chopped flat-leaf parsley
freshly ground black pepper
12 whole sage leaves
200 g buffalo-milk mozzarella, broken into pieces

Preheat the oven to 180°C. Roast the whole eggplants for 10 minutes or until soft, then remove from the oven and set aside until cool enough to handle. Cut in half and scoop out the softened flesh. Set aside. Blanch the asparagus spears in boiling salted water for 10 minutes. Drain and cut the spears in half crosswise.

Lift the mushrooms from their soaking water and squeeze. Heat 50 ml olive oil in a large frying pan and sauté the mushrooms and garlic for 3 minutes. Add the sage and parsley. Season to taste with salt and pepper and add the asparagus. Sauté for 2–3 minutes. Add the eggplant and toss, allowing it to break up roughly and heat through. Remove the pan from the heat. Spoon the vegetables onto serving plates and drizzle with the pan juices. Allow to cool a little. Meanwhile, in a separate pan, heat a little olive oil. Fry the sage leaves briefly until crisp, then drain on kitchen paper. Scatter the mozzarella and fried sage leaves over and serve warm. *Serves 4*

Note: Both Italian porcini – known in France as *cèpes* – and Australian slippery jacks are mushrooms from the *Boletus* genus. They have a similar appearance, texture and flavour, but slippery jacks do not share the flavour characteristics that make porcini and *cèpes* such prized culinary ingredients. Porcini are most easily obtained in their dried state, although they are sometimes available frozen from specialist food stores. Frozen porcini simply need to be defrosted and cut to the required size. Very occasionally freshly imported porcini or *cèpes* pop up in the market – if you come across them, they are well worth buying.

2 × 1 kg farmed rabbits
(see Note)
1 onion, finely chopped
2 sticks celery, finely chopped
1 medium carrot, finely chopped
2 cloves garlic, finely chopped
¼ cup finely chopped thyme
leaves from 1 sprig rosemary,
finely chopped
2 cups white wine
2 cups Chicken Stock
(see page 20)
100 ml olive oil
sea salt
freshly cracked black pepper
6 leaves gelatine (10 g in total)
½ cup freshly chopped
flat-leaf parsley
300 g pâté-style *or*
1 lobe duck foie gras (see
Note), cut into 1 cm thick slices
6 handfuls mâche
(lamb's lettuce) leaves

### Spiced figs
24 ripe figs
2 cups port
500 ml red wine
6 cloves
1 star anise

# Sformato di coniglio con fichi

RABBIT AND FOIE GRAS TERRINE WITH SPICED FIGS

Preheat the oven to 200°C. Break the rabbits into joints and put them into a roasting tray. Scatter over the onion, celery, carrot, garlic, thyme and rosemary, then pour in the wine, stock and olive oil. Season to taste with salt and pepper and massage the rabbit pieces with the liquid and seasonings. Roast for 25 minutes, turning and tossing the meat and vegetables from time to time.

Remove from the oven and allow to cool slightly. Lift out the rabbit pieces, reserving all the vegetables and roasting juices. Tear off the meat and discard the bones, then roughly chop the meat and return it to the roasting tray. Strain 2 cups of the roasting juices, then add the gelatine leaves and stir to dissolve. Tip into the tray. Add the parsley and check for seasoning.

Lightly oil a terrine mould and line the bottom and sides with plastic wrap, leaving some hanging outside the mould ready to be folded over the finished terrine. Arrange the foie gras in the bottom of the mould, then fill the mould with the rabbit mixture. Fold the overlapping plastic wrap over the terrine to seal well. Place a light weight on top and refrigerate overnight.

To make the spiced figs, put all the ingredients in a saucepan and cook over a moderate heat for 15 minutes, stirring occasionally.

When ready to serve, unwrap the terrine and carefully invert it onto a board. Lift off the mould and remove the plastic wrap. Using a sharp knife, cut the terrine into 1 cm slices. Serve each person with a slice of terrine, 2 spiced figs and some mâche leaves.   *Serves 12*

Note: As a general rule I prefer to use farmed rabbit, as the quality of the meat is assured. Your butcher will be able to supply this. The dish works with chicken, too. Do try to include the foie gras, but if you cannot find it, leave it out. Foie gras, meaning 'fat liver', is called *fegato grasso* in Italian. The method of production is prohibited in Australia, so true foie gras is only available imported from France. Further local regulations state that imported foie gras must have been pasteurised to a certain temperature, which means that the raw preserved lobe of the liver is unavailable here. I have found that the pasteurised lobe yields excellent results when sliced, quickly pan-fried and splashed with Sauternes. 'Pâté-style' foie gras, shaped into a loaf or log, can also be purchased, and although it is made of offcuts the quality is good and perfectly suitable for dishes such as this terrine.

*Wow! How good can meat get? Wagyu, from the breed of cattle used in Japan for the famous Kobe beef, is becoming more accessible in Australia. This recipe was inspired by an old northern Italian dish called* carne albese, *which used raw beef long before beef* carpaccio *was invented. Thin slivers of raw wagyu (or other best-quality beef) are served with lovely, fresh julienned apple and dressed with a little olive oil, a bit of truffle and a couple of drops of* vincotto. *Add an egg and some seasoning and pop it on a plate, perhaps with some fresh green leaves – beautiful!*

# Carne con vincotto e cicoria

## RAW WAGYU WITH VINCOTTO AND CHICORY

6 eggs
300 g wagyu beef fillet
    (*or* other best-quality beef;
    *see* Note)
sea salt
freshly ground black pepper
1½ tablespoons vincotto
    (see page 40)
2 tablespoons olive oil
1 teaspoon freshly chopped
    flat-leaf parsley
1 Granny Smith apple, unpeeled
shavings of fresh black *or*
    white truffle (to taste) *or*
    a few drops of truffle oil
4 ripe figs, thinly sliced
1 generous handful chicory leaves

Separate the eggs, putting each egg yolk into a separate cup. Reserve the whites for another use.

Cut the beef into thin strips, then transfer to a large bowl and season to taste with salt and pepper. Add 2 egg yolks and the *vincotto*, olive oil and parsley and toss well until the meat is glossy and the egg has been incorporated. Cut the apple into thin julienne and add to the beef with the truffle shavings, tossing gently to combine evenly.

Arrange the fig slices on each plate. Top with a serving of beef and then 1 egg yolk. Put the chicory leaves in a bowl and drizzle with olive oil. Arrange the dressed leaves alongside the beef and serve.   *Serves 4*

Note: The area surrounding the Japanese city of Kobe has been producing wagyu beef for many years. Genuine Kobe beef is extremely expensive. Much of its high price relates to land and breeding costs rather than to the quality of the meat itself. The beef is now being grown in Australia, and ironically, much of the wagyu produced here is exported to Japan and processed in Kobe. Other high-quality beef can be substituted for wagyu, such as good, fat-marbled ox beef.

# Salads

I think salads are fantastic, and a lot of the time there's not enough attention paid to them, with people tending to throw a salad together as an afterthought. I love a really simple crisp and fresh iceberg lettuce salad with a few red onion slices tossed through it. It becomes a vehicle to carry really good olive oil and a splash of vinegar.

But you can make some wonderfully different salads, and they can be elevated to different levels depending on the ingredients you use. You can cut fine slivers of fennel and dress them with olive oil and a touch of chilli, pop in some orange segments and radicchio leaves, and you have another dimension of flavour. It's a simple salad, with that lovely freshness, crunch and crispness.

Salad is a cleansing experience. It leaves the palate nice and refreshed, especially with a bit of vinegar – the acid cleans everything up. I always wait till I finish my meat dish to grab the salad and hop into it, because I love leaving my mouth feeling really fresh. And let's face it, it's really healthy to fill up on salad rather then reaching for another piece of meat.

Salads can be considered as dishes on their own, but some work better as side dishes to main courses. For example, the fennel salad I mentioned above would be perfect with fish or pork. (Often you see pork sausages with fennel seeds through them at the butcher, because it's a flavour combination that seems to work well.) There's no need to get too pedantic or fussy about marrying the right type of salad with the right main course – you'll spend half the day worrying rather than preparing the salad! Giving it a bit of thought is good, but so is getting on with it.

*The aniseedy fennel is the star here, while the bitter radicchio duels with the sweetness of the orange. This salad reminds me of my mother – I'm not sure whether that is because it uses radicchio, which is very popular in her home town of Verona, or because its flavour is both sweet and sharp, like her personality!*

1 head Treviso radicchio
    (see Note)
1 bulb fennel, finely sliced
1 orange
1 tablespoon finely chopped
    flat-leaf parsley
½ fresh chilli,
    seeded and chopped
juice of 1 lemon
sea salt
freshly ground black pepper
100 ml extra-virgin olive oil

# Insalata di finocchio e arancia

## FENNEL AND ORANGE SALAD

Separate the radicchio leaves and wash them well. Put the leaves into a serving bowl and add the fennel.

Using a sharp knife, remove the peel and pith from the orange, then carefully separate each segment from the membrane.

Add the orange segments to the salad, then stir in the parsley, chilli and lemon juice. Season well with salt and pepper and drizzle with the olive oil. Toss to combine, and serve.   *Serves 2–4*

Note: Treviso radicchio has long leaves with a more delicate flavour than the rounder-leafed variety. I prefer to use Treviso radicchio for this salad, but round-leafed radicchio works just as well.

*I love serving potato salad when people come around. You can dress this version with a light mayonnaise, or even just some olive oil, lemon juice and parsley. It's a classic preparation that depends on the seasoning and the flavour of the vegetables. Kohlrabi is a fantastic, under-utilised root vegetable that looks kind of like a big turnip, but tastes more like a cabbage. Make a bit of an effort choosing the potatoes, because decent ones do make a difference. There are lots of different varieties out there – Spunta, King Edward, Desiree – and it's great that our selection has come such a long way and we have a choice.*

# Insalata di patate e cavolrape

## POTATO AND KOHLRABI SALAD

800 g waxy potatoes
    (see Note)
1 kohlrabi
2 egg yolks
1 teaspoon Dijon mustard
200 ml white-wine vinegar
sea salt
freshly ground black pepper
300 ml olive oil
½ cup freshly snipped chives

Put the whole potatoes and kohlrabi into a pot and cover with water. Bring to the boil and simmer for 20 minutes or until the potatoes are tender when pierced with a skewer. Remove the potatoes and drain. Cook the kohlrabi for a further 10 minutes or until tender, then drain. Allow the vegetables to cool for about 30 minutes or until you can handle them comfortably – they should still be warm. Using a small knife, peel the potatoes and kohlrabi and cut into 2 cm cubes. Put them into a serving bowl and set aside.

Combine the egg yolks, mustard and vinegar in an electric blender, then season to taste with salt and pepper. Blend in the olive oil a little at a time until it has all been incorporated. Pour the dressing over the vegetables. Add the chives and toss to combine. Let the salad stand for 1 hour before serving to allow the flavours to incorporate.   Serves 6

Note: For a salad such as this, I would choose a solid, waxy potato with a bit of butteriness about it so it's got a bit of depth in its flavour, and a good compact consistency so it won't fall apart. Spunta potatoes, or even kipflers, are ideal.

*I don't like to say what my favourite foods are because if I single out one or two I feel I am being unfaithful to the others. The truth is I love them all! But this simple home-style tomato and red onion salad – wow! It's very Italian, in the sense that it's simple and a lot of people make it at home.*

## Insalata di pomodoro e cipolla

### TOMATO AND ONION SALAD

4 ripe tomatoes
½ red onion, finely sliced
1 teaspoon fresh oregano leaves
1 tablespoon freshly chopped
    flat-leaf parsley
100 ml extra-virgin olive oil
50 ml white-wine vinegar
sea salt
freshly ground black pepper

If you prefer, peel and core the tomatoes. Cut the tomatoes into wedges and put into a serving bowl. Add the remaining ingredients and mix well. Allow to stand for 15 minutes before serving.

Note: This salad relies on the quality of the tomatoes used, and the quest for beautiful-flavoured, earth-grown tomatoes is becoming more and more difficult. Use best-quality ripe tomatoes with a full flavour – I suggest oxhearts if you can get them.

*Mushrooms can appear throughout most of the menu. This is a simple way of presenting your favourite kind of mushroom as a side dish or even as a first course. Include as many or as few varieties as you like. Yum!*

## Insalata di funghi

### MUSHROOM SALAD

500 g assorted field mushrooms,
    sliced
200 ml olive oil
50 ml red-wine vinegar *or*
    balsamic vinegar
1 clove garlic, finely sliced
1 tablespoon freshly chopped
    flat-leaf parsley
sea salt
freshly ground black pepper

Heat 50 ml of the olive oil in a large frying pan. Sauté the mushrooms for about 5 minutes, then transfer to a bowl. Add the remaining ingredients and toss to combine. Serve at room temperature.   *Serves 4–6*

*Opposite:* Insalata di Pomodoro e Cipolla

*Panzanella is a delightful, fresh-tasting, summery Tuscan salad. Whenever we put it on the menu at the restaurant it is very popular as an entrée. It also works well as a palate-cleanser after a meat dish – maybe grilled Tuscan-style beef or lamb chops.*

# Panzanella

### TUSCAN BREAD AND TOMATO SALAD

½ loaf stale Italian-style bread (see Note)
4 very large, ripe tomatoes
1 clove garlic, finely sliced
½ cup extra-virgin olive oil
½ cup balsamic vinegar
1 large red onion, finely sliced
6 fresh basil leaves, sliced *or* left whole if small
1 tablespoon fresh oregano leaves
sea salt
freshly cracked black pepper

Preheat the oven to 150°C. Remove and discard the crusts from the bread. Cut the bread into 3 cm cubes and spread them on a baking tray. Dry in the oven for about 15 minutes until crisp. Allow to cool.

Cut the tomatoes into 3 cm cubes. In a large bowl, combine the garlic, olive oil and vinegar. Add the bread and toss to coat.

Add the onion, basil and oregano and season to taste with salt and pepper. Add the tomato and toss gently. Set aside for 30 minutes before serving to let the flavours infuse.   *Serves 6*

Note: The bread in this recipe needs to be quite dry and stale. The best kind is a heavy, dense, crusty loaf that will assist in soaking up the flavoursome liquids. Be sure to use the best tomatoes and balsamic vinegar you can buy.

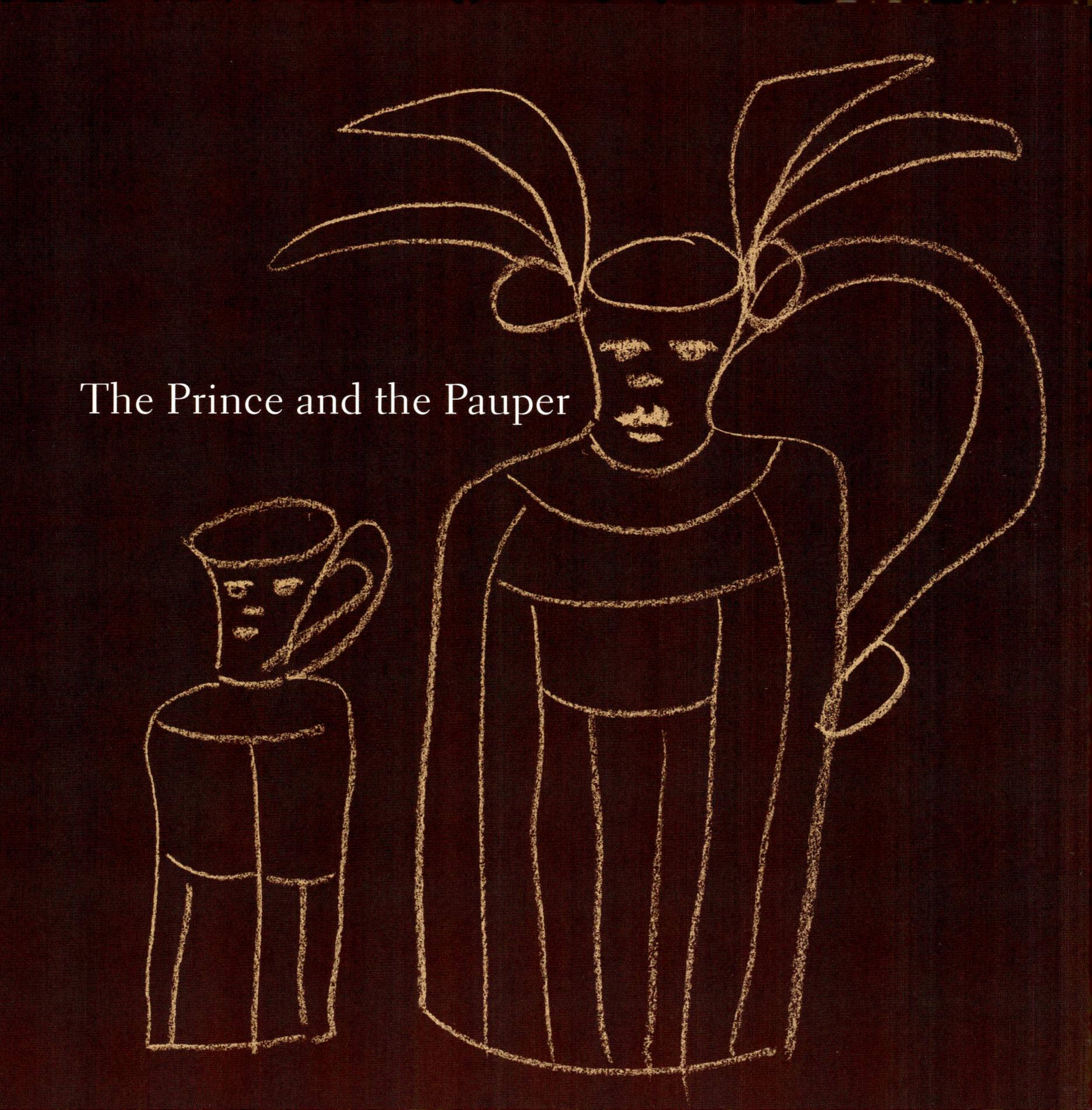

When I was thinking about pasta and soup for this book, I kept coming back to the idea that while both pasta and soup come from simple peasant backgrounds, you can also make them very extravagant, depending on your ingredients and preparation. They can be both a prince and a pauper.

Think of a beautiful soup boiling away with potatoes, turnips and other vegetables that were available to people without the means for any more elaborate ingredients, such as meat. Pasta is much the same: just flour and water mixed together to make a dough, used to add bulk to a meal. But each can also be dressed up so that it comes out as a very elegant, sometimes very costly dish, like the *bigoli* I've included here (see page 62), which is a pasta dish with roast potatoes and truffles. Both of these grow in the ground – the princely truffle and the humble potato – so they're connected for me, and in this wonderful dish their flavours sit well together.

I've covered quite a few pasta-making techniques in this section. The ingredients given for the fillings and sauces are suggestions only, and are there for you to use your imagination and adapt or substitute to create dishes of your own. They require a bit of practice and experience in the kitchen – you might do a few dodgy ravioli to start off – but once you've grasped the concept of the folding (and it's not rocket science!), your pasta will get better and better. Then, once you've got the main concept of making a filling (it can't be too wet, or it'll go straight through the pasta) – well, the world's your oyster and you can create anything you like. You'll see things and think, 'That would be great in a ravioli filling', and you'll try it with confidence.

Same with the soups. There are some classic preparations that have been done a certain way for centuries – but with these as your base, doors will open and you'll see other things that would work. For example, you can use cauliflower for a beautiful creamed cauliflower soup, but you could also use Jerusalem artichokes or asparagus. The list is endless. Once you've mastered the techniques, you can just go for it.

## Pasta Fresca

Pasta is a beautiful section of the Italian kitchen, centuries old. It started with the ancient Romans putting together very primitive flour-and-water doughs and drying them for use in big spicy soups and casseroles. Don't let people tell you pasta was brought from China by Marco Polo. The ancient Chinese were making a type of noodle also, but as an Italian boy I'm here to say that my people have always worked with some sort of dough!

I have grown up with making pasta. My mother often had our kitchen bench totally covered with flour and the dining-room table laden with white tablecloths, covering layers of freshly rolled pasta. I would take up my seat on the other side of the bench and watch her nimble fingers magically turning little balls of white dough into small, hat-like shapes with a quick push and twist. In no time, the tray to her left would be covered in hundreds of *cappelletti*. My mouth would begin to water because I knew that in a short amount of time they would be cooked and covered in *sugo*, her sauce, which was simmering on the stove behind her.

Having a mother from the north of Italy, I was privy to the gnocchi-making process, as well as numerous pasta shapes and flavours. I also had the advantage of learning from my father, who was born in the south and was a cook by trade. I learned a great deal about southern flavours, and I like to use the methods in the kitchen today, both at home and in the restaurant. My mother, Marisa (or Gabriela as she is known to close friends and as my father preferred to call her), most often served gnocchi with a simple *salsa di pomodoro* (see page 18), but they are also delicious with *matriciana* sauce (see 130). Another simple way of serving gnocchi – and arguably the most delicious – is *al burro e salvia*: with sage leaves crisped in nut-brown butter, topped with shaved Parmigiano-Reggiano. *Buonissimo!*

Making your own pasta can be very rewarding. Once you've made a few ravioli and tortellini and you start to get the hang of it, it's quite satisfying to see the production coming along. Making pasta is such a beautifully communal activity, too. It can be a lot of fun for people to make together – somebody fills the tortellini, somebody folds them. At home, I love having the kids in the kitchen helping me make it. My daughter loves to put her fingers into the flour and try her hand at shaping pasta. I think she also loves the experience of knowing that her plate will soon be filled with freshly made pasta or gnocchi, glistening in the sauce we both love so much. Handmade and turned pasta may be more time-consuming, but the end product is elegant and the effort is certainly worth it.

Some people seem to think that fresh pasta is better than dry pasta, but it's not as simple as that. They're different products, made and used differently, and tasting different too. You can find poor fresh

pasta as well as good fresh pasta, and the same is true of dry pasta. (See the 'Improvviso' chapter for more about dry pastas.)

The quality of pasta matters. If you're doing a spaghetti dish with, say, *aiolio* – which is just garlic, olive oil, parsley and seasoning – a high-quality dry pasta is essential to make it something special. For the difference in money between a good dry pasta and a cheap one that's not so good, I'd go for a good pasta every time, such as the Martelli brand I love to buy. It's only a few bucks at the end of the day, and it's not like you're buying tons of it. Once you've tried really high-quality dry pasta, you'll be converted. It stays firmer for longer in the water and doesn't overcook as easily, and it's got a lovely bite to it.

You must have plenty of boiling water when you cook pasta. Sometimes I see people with a little pot and they want to put in a big handful of pasta. Because of the flour content, they end up with a gluggy mess. It doesn't cook nicely loose and fresh, and it doesn't seal in that lovely floury flavour. The water has to be well salted as well, because salt helps to retain the natural flavour in the pasta. Don't worry about over-salting the water – there's nothing worse than insipid, bland pasta, which also means your sauce has to work harder. If the pasta is tasty already, then the sauce acts as a beautiful dressing for it.

Whatever the pasta, it's best served immediately after cooking. I remember my mother used to call out 'Butto la pasta!', which means, 'I'm putting in the pasta!' Once she was putting the pasta in the water, that was it – it came out and it was ready on the table. If you didn't turn up in time, it was your own bad luck. You had overcooked, soggy pasta, and no one to blame but yourself.

Get the pasta out of the boiling water, strain it, dress it and serve it. Sometimes people refresh it in water and reheat it later, but really, you should cook it when you need it. If for some reason you need to pre-cook pasta for later, never wash it under cold water as you'll be washing all the starch and the delightful flavour down the sink. To prepare it for later (especially dry pasta), cook it to halfway ready, then take it out of the boiling water, drain it and spread it out on a tray so that it cools quickly and stops cooking. You can even pop it into the fridge for a few minutes. Then, when you're ready, warm it up again and put it into your sauce to finish cooking.

*Bigoli is a very old style of Venetian pasta. The dough has butter and milk in it, which softens it and results in pasta with a richer flavour than the normal variety.*

1 onion, finely chopped
1 clove garlic, chopped
2 large waxy potatoes, peeled and thinly sliced
½ teaspoon freshly chopped rosemary
½ teaspoon freshly chopped sage
sea salt
freshly ground black pepper
50 ml olive oil
1 cup Chicken Stock (see page 20)
2 tablespoons freshly grated Parmigiano-Reggiano
shavings of fresh black or white truffle (to taste) *or* a few drops of truffle oil

*Bigoli*
300 g flour
pinch of salt
100 g softened butter
1 egg, lightly beaten
¼ cup milk

# Bigoli con patate e tartufi

## BIGOLI WITH POTATO AND TRUFFLE

To make the *bigoli*, put the flour on a clean work surface and sprinkle with the salt. Gently rub the butter into the flour until it resembles breadcrumbs. Make a well in the centre and add the egg and milk. Knead for about 10 minutes until smooth. Roll out the dough into 3–4 sheets about 3 mm thick, then cut into spaghetti-like lengths using a *chitarra* or pizza wheel. Spread the *bigoli* on a floured tray and cover with a clean tea towel. Set aside.

Preheat the oven to 180°C. Scatter the onion and garlic in a baking dish. Cover with the potato and sprinkle with the herbs. Add salt and pepper to taste. Pour over the olive oil and stock, and sprinkle with the cheese. Bake for 20 minutes or until the potato is soft.

Bring a large pot of salted water to the boil. Cook the *bigoli* for 3 minutes, then drain. Return to the pot with the contents of the baking dish and toss to combine. Serve garnished with shaved truffle to taste, or drizzled with truffle oil.   Serves 4

Note: I use a tool from Abruzzo called a *chitarra* (so-called because of its steel strings – *chitarra* means 'guitar') to cut the pasta (see picture on page 60). You can purchase them at Italian speciality stores such as Melbourne's Enoteca Sileno.

*This is one of those dishes I love to prepare with my children. Somehow the flour always ends up all over the kitchen and all over us. Gorgonzola is smelly and punchy and is great with homemade gnocchi.*

# Gnocchi gorgonzola

## GNOCCHI WITH GORGONZOLA SAUCE

2.5 kg waxy potatoes, washed but unpeeled
5 egg yolks
440 g flour

*Gorgonzola sauce*
200 g dolce latte gorgonzola (*see* Note), broken into pieces
½ cup cream
½ cup freshly grated Parmigiano-Reggiano
sea salt
freshly cracked black pepper

To make the gorgonzola sauce, combine all the ingredients in a saucepan. Bring to a simmer and reduce until creamy (this will take about 5 minutes). Keep warm until ready to serve.

Bring a large pot of water to the boil. Cook the potatoes until tender, then refresh immediately in cold water and peel. Bring a fresh pot of lightly salted water to the boil. Meanwhile, pass the potatoes through a potato ricer onto your work surface until well mashed. Add the eggs and flour and knead until well blended. Using your hands, roll the mixture into thin 'sausages' about 2 cm thick, then cut the sausages into small pieces. Roll each piece over the tines of a fork to create the traditional groove marks. Drop the gnocchi into the boiling water in small batches. Remove them when they rise to the surface (about 2 minutes) and transfer to a large dish to keep warm. Repeat with the remaining gnocchi.

Pour the gorgonzola sauce onto the cooked gnocchi and toss until well coated. Serve immediately.   *Serves 8*

Note: *Dolce latte* gorgonzola is creamier and less piquant than other types of gorgonzola such as gorgonzola *piccante* (meaning piquant) and gorgonzola *dolce verde* (meaning sweet). You can find these cheeses at good delicatessens and specialist food stores.

*This tasty dish relies on the delicate flavour of the broad beans bound with the ricotta. The cherry tomatoes give extra sweetness. I love broad beans because they remind me of my childhood, when there were always broad beans growing in the backyard. Dad used to love eating them raw out of the pods, but we'd also braise them.*

# Ravioli di fave con pomodorini

## BROAD-BEAN RAVIOLI WITH CHERRY TOMATO SAUCE

flour
500 g Fresh Pasta Dough
    (see page 21)
100 g butter
6 fresh sage leaves, chopped
sea salt
freshly ground black pepper
½ cup freshly grated Parmigiano-
    Reggiano

*Filling*
250 g fresh broad beans, shelled
250 g ricotta
sea salt
freshly ground black pepper

*Cherry tomato sauce*
50 ml olive oil
250 g shallots, finely sliced
1 clove garlic, chopped
1 teaspoon freshly chopped
    marjoram
1 teaspoon freshly chopped
    oregano
1 cup basil leaves
sea salt
freshly ground black pepper
200 g tomato paste
300 g cherry tomatoes
2 cups Vegetable Stock
    (see page 20)
½ cup freshly chopped
    flat-leaf parsley

To make the filling, bring a large pot of salted water to the boil. Add the broad beans. When the water returns to the boil, remove the beans and refresh quickly in cold water. Slip each bean out of its tough second skin. Set aside a small handful of beans for the garnish. Purée half the remaining beans until smooth, then add the remaining beans and purée roughly, so that some texture is retained. Transfer the bean purée to a large bowl and blend in an equal amount of ricotta. Season to taste with salt and pepper.

Scatter a clean work surface with flour and roll out the pasta into 2 very thin 8 cm × 60 cm sheets. Put a spoonful of filling in one row every 4 cm or so along each sheet of pasta (15 spoonfuls per sheet). Brush one long edge of each sheet with a little water, then fold the pasta over the filling and press down firmly around the filling to seal, expelling any air bubbles. Using a crinkle-edged cutter, cut between each pocket of mixture to create 30 individual ravioli.

To make the cherry tomato sauce, heat the olive oil in a large frying pan. Add the shallots and garlic, then stir in the marjoram, oregano and half the basil leaves. Season to taste with salt and pepper. Cook gently for 10 minutes or until the shallots are very tender. Stir in the tomato paste and cook for 2 minutes until deepened in colour (caramelised). Add the cherry tomatoes and pour in the stock to just cover the vegetables. Simmer gently for 20 minutes. Some of the cherry tomatoes should break up and some should remain whole. Stir in the parsley and the remaining basil.

Bring a large pot of salted water to a vigorous boil. Tip in the ravioli and cook for 4 minutes, then drain. Melt the butter in a small frying pan. Add the sage and the reserved broad beans, then season to taste with salt and pepper. Add the ravioli and toss to coat. Sprinkle with Parmigiano-Reggiano and serve immediately, offering the cherry tomato sauce separately so your guests can add their own desired amount.   *Serves 4*

*This dish is typical of Carusino, my father's home town in the Taranto province of Puglia, an ancient region rich in agriculture. I can smell the local soil as I write. Dishes of pasta mixed with fresh vegetables are prominent in the* cucina. Orecchiette *can be dressed with many different sauces, but broccoli raab – a fantastic green vegetable – is a classic. If it is not in season, use broccoli or silver beet for excellent results.*

# Orecchiette con cime di rapa

## EAR-SHAPED PASTA WITH BROCCOLI RAAB

500 g white flour
500 g wholemeal flour
salt
1 cup water
4 kipfler potatoes,
    washed but unpeeled
200 g broccoli raab,
    washed and trimmed
2 tablespoons olive oil
200 g cured pork cheek
    (see Note), sliced
2 cloves garlic, finely chopped
1 fresh red chilli, seeded
    and finely chopped
2 teaspoons Basil Pesto
    (see page 18)
freshly ground black pepper
handful of freshly grated pecorino
    or Parmigiano-Reggiano
generous pinch of finely chopped
    flat-leaf parsley

*Variation: For a simpler, lighter version of the dish, blanch the broccoli raab in boiling salted water, then use the same water to boil the pasta. Drain the pasta and put it into a bowl with the broccoli raab. Drizzle with lots of excellent olive oil, season with salt and pepper and enjoy.*

Mix the flours in a bowl with a good pinch of salt. Make a well in the centre and pour in the water. Mix well with a wooden spoon until the mixture forms a firm ball (you may need to add more water). Transfer the dough to your workbench and knead it for 10 minutes until smooth and elastic. Break off a fist-sized piece of dough and shape it into a long, thin log 1 cm in diameter. Cut the log into 1 cm pieces. Repeat with remaining dough. Push the flat blade down of a butter knife into each small piece of dough until it curls over the sides of the blade to make an 'ear' shape. Put the *orecchiette* onto a floured tray and set aside.

Put the potatoes into a saucepan of lightly salted cold water. Bring to the boil and cook until tender. Drain. Peel and dice when cool enough to handle. Set aside.

Bring a large pot of lightly salted water to the boil. Strip the leaves from the broccoli raab and cut the stems into 3 cm pieces. Boil the stems, uncovered, for 8–10 minutes. Add the leaves and cook for 3–4 minutes, then drain and set aside. Bring a fresh pot of salted water to the boil. Meanwhile, heat the olive oil in a large frying pan. Sauté the reserved potato and the pork cheek until crisp, then add the garlic, chilli, pesto and broccoli raab stems and leaves. Sauté until the broccoli raab is heated through. Keep warm until ready to serve.

Tip the *orecchiette* into the boiling water and cook for 5–8 minutes until al dente. Drain, then add to the frying pan with the vegetables. Season to taste with salt and pepper, then add the pecorino and parsley and toss to distribute evenly. If it looks a little dry, stir in some olive oil. Serve immediately.    Serves 4

Note: Cured pork cheek is air-dried in the same way as prosciutto, and has a similar appearance. However, it has more fat and a richer texture than prosciutto. It's fantastic for bruschetta. It is worth seeking out an Italian butcher if you want to obtain pork cheek for this dish, but you can substitute pancetta or speck. Alternatively, you could omit the pork cheek.

*I would always look forward to 'cannelloni day' when I was a boy. There was a sense of occasion that was almost festive, and my mamma always managed something delizioso. What you use for your cannelloni filling is limited only by your imagination or what you happen to have in the kitchen. Yesterday's leftover roast is fantastic, as are vegetarian fillings such as spinach and ricotta. Here I combine rabbit with gamey tastes and rich wild mushrooms – so homely.*

# Cannelloni di coniglio con funghi

RABBIT CANNELLONI WITH WILD MUSHROOM SAUCE

500 g Fresh Pasta Dough
    (*see* page 21)
water
olive oil
salt

*Wild mushroom sauce*
50 ml olive oil
1 onion, finely chopped
2 cloves garlic, finely chopped
½ cup tomato paste
100 g mixed dried mushrooms,
    soaked overnight
1 cup red wine
1 litre Chicken Stock
    (see page 20)
salt
freshly ground black pepper
2 tablespoons freshly chopped
    flat-leaf parsley

To make the wild mushroom sauce, heat the oil in a heavy-based saucepan. Add the onions and garlic and sauté over a medium heat for 3–5 minutes until golden. Add the tomato paste and cook for 5 minutes, stirring so that the paste does not stick or burn. Remove the mushrooms from their soaking liquid and add them to the saucepan. Cook for 3 minutes, stirring well. Pour in the red wine and stock and season to taste with salt and pepper. Add the parsley and reduce the heat. Simmer for 30 minutes, uncovered, stirring occasionally.

Meanwhile, make the rabbit filling (*see* over for ingredients). Preheat the oven to 180°C. Chop the rabbit into pieces and transfer to a roasting tray. Add the vegetables, herbs and juniper berries. Season to taste with salt and pepper. Pour in the oil and white wine, then massage the rabbit pieces with the liquids and seasonings. Roast for about 30 minutes, mixing occasionally, until the meat is golden and cooked through. Remove the tray from the oven (leave the oven on) and lift the rabbit pieces onto a rack. When it is cool enough to handle, tear off the meat, making sure all small bones are removed. Discard the bones and return the meat to the roasting tray. Tear the bread into pieces and mix with the meat. Pass the mixture through the large holes of a mincer, then transfer it to the bowl of an electric mixer. Add the egg and Parmigiano-Reggiano and mix well. The mixture should be firm yet moist. ▶

*Rabbit filling*

1 × 1–1.2 kg farmed rabbit
1 onion, roughly chopped
½ carrot, roughly chopped
1 stick celery, roughly chopped
¼ leek, roughly chopped
2 cloves garlic, chopped
1 teaspoon freshly chopped rosemary
1 teaspoon freshly chopped sage
3 juniper berries, crushed
salt
freshly ground black pepper
100 ml olive oil
300 ml white wine
2–3 slices day-old bread, crusts removed
1 egg
1 cup freshly grated Parmigiano-Reggiano

Roll out the pasta very finely into 2 × 12 cm wide sheets, then cut each sheet into four 12 cm squares. Have ready a large bowl of cold water with a splash of olive oil in it. Bring a large pot of salted water to the boil. Cook the pasta sheets in batches (3–4 at a time) for 2 minutes, then lift out and transfer immediately to the bowl of cold water. Lift the sheets from the cold water 3–4 at a time and lay them out on your work surface.

Oil a baking tray well. Spoon the rabbit filling into a piping bag, then pipe a 'sausage' of filling about 3 cm in diameter down the length of each pasta sheet. Roll the pasta around the filling and put the cannelloni, seam-side down, into the prepared baking tray. Cover with the wild mushroom sauce and bake for 15 minutes. Serve immediately.   *Serves 4*

*This pasta sauce is rich and luscious. Don't go there if you're looking for something light! I must tell you that after you have tried it you will be seduced forever. I love it so much that sometimes I can't wait for the pasta to cook and go ahead and eat a bowl of the sauce with some bread!*

150 ml olive oil
1 onion, finely chopped
1 clove garlic,
   crushed and chopped
1 fresh red chilli,
   seeded and finely chopped
1 tablespoon finely chopped
   fresh coriander
½ cup finely chopped
   flat-leaf parsley
½ cup tomato paste
2 tablespoons plain flour
150 ml white wine
½ litre water *or* Fish Stock
   (*see* page 20)
sea salt
freshly ground black pepper
1 kg fresh calamari, cleaned
1–1.5 kg tagliarini (*see* Note)

# Tagliarini con sugo di calamari

## TAGLIARINI WITH CALAMARI SAUCE

Heat one third of the olive oil in a frying pan and fry the onion, garlic and chilli until the onion is translucent. Add the herbs and fry for about 5 minutes, stirring, until the onion is golden. Add the tomato paste and flour and cook for 2–3 minutes until the tomato paste deepens in colour (caramelises). Deglaze the pan with the white wine and allow to reduce for 3–4 minutes. Add the water and season to taste with salt and pepper. Set aside and keep warm.

Cut the calamari bodies into 1 cm × 5 cm strips and the tentacles into 5 cm bunches. Heat the remaining olive oil in a separate large pan and fry the calamari in 2–3 batches until golden, then drain on kitchen paper. Add the calamari to the sauce and simmer gently for 30–40 minutes. Set aside and keep warm.

Bring a large pot of salted water to the boil and add the tagliarini. Cook until al dente, then drain. Return the pasta to the pot. Stir through 2–3 large spoonfuls of the sauce. Serve the pasta with a generous spoonful of sauce on top for each diner.   *Serves 10*

Note: This recipe is excellent for a larger gathering. The sauce will keep for up to 3 days in the refrigerator, and also freezes well. Tagliarini is a thin, long, flat pasta similar to linguine. Any flat long pasta works for this dish. Cuttlefish could be substituted for the calamari.

*I designed this unusual dish for a special dinner held in honour of the great pioneer Melbourne chef Hermann Schneider. It depends strongly on fundamental skills and techniques, executed with care and passion – all the good things Mr Schneider taught. He ran South Yarra's famous Two Faces restaurant with his family for twenty-seven years before moving on to Delgany at Portsea. As a young chef I was fortunate to work under him, and have remained in contact ever since. He trained his people well, utilising discipline and passion in a quest for something better than ordinary. Australia's culinary scene is indebted to him.*

# Ravioli di midollo

## BONE-MARROW RAVIOLI

500 g Fresh Pasta Dough
    (*see* page 21)
flour
salt
1 cup Demi-glace (*see* page 19)
olive oil
4 asparagus spears, peeled
    and finely sliced lengthways
4 slices black or white truffle *or*
    a few drops of truffle oil (optional)

*Filling*
2 kg marrow bones,
    cut into small pieces (*see* Note)
water
½ loaf stale Italian-style bread,
    crusts removed
½ clove garlic, finely chopped
1 teaspoon freshly chopped sage
1 teaspoon freshly chopped rosemary
grated zest of 1 lemon
2 tablespoons freshly grated
    Parmigiano-Reggiano
1 egg
sea salt
freshly ground black pepper
breadcrumbs

To make the filling, put the marrow bones into a large pot and cover with water. Bring to the boil and cook for 5 minutes, then drain and allow to cool. Push out the marrow from the bones into a bowl (you will end up with about 500 g bone marrow). Discard the bones. Break the bread into pieces, then soak it for 2–3 minutes in enough water to cover. Squeeze out any excess liquid and add an equal quantity of bread to the marrow. Add the garlic, herbs, lemon zest, Parmigiano-Reggiano and egg. Season to taste with salt and pepper. Put the mixture into the bowl of an electric mixer fitted with a heavy paddle beater. Mix on medium speed until well incorporated and firm yet moist. If the mixture is too wet, adjust it with dried breadcrumbs.

Roll out the pasta dough very thinly into 6 × 8 cm × 60 cm sheets. Laying the sheets on a lightly floured work surface, put spoonfuls of the mixture every 4 cm or so along each sheet. Brush one long edge of each sheet with water, then fold it over the filling and push down to expel any air bubbles. Press firmly to seal. Using a crinkle-edged cutter, cut between each pocket of mixture to create individual ravioli.

Bring a large pot of salted water to the boil. Meanwhile, gently heat the demi-glace until hot. Cook the ravioli in the boiling water for 3–4 minutes, then drain. Lightly dress the ravioli with olive oil and divide between serving plates. Garnish with the raw asparagus and the truffle, if using. Drizzle liberally with the demi-glace and serve.   *Serves 6*

Note: Ask your butcher to cut the marrow bones into pieces for you.

# Zuppa

People know straight away when you've got a soup on the go. You've got the pot on, things are roasting up and cooking away – it makes it feel like home when that aroma is going through the house.

There are very simple soups, like *stracciatella*, with chicken broth and egg (see page 78), but I've also included some heavier, more elaborate recipes here. The stunning roasted chestnut and mushroom soup (page 82), a rich Tuscan-style preparation, has a wonderful aroma that fills the room. As mushrooms and chestnuts become available at the same time, this is a special dish full of autumn and winter flavours.

The quality of the base ingredient in soups is very important. If you're making something like *stracciatella*, you're depending on really good chicken stock because it's what supports the soup and there's not much to mask its flavour. For the chestnut and mushroom soup, it's all about cooking the onion and the vegetables nice and slowly in the bottom of the pot at the beginning, getting them to caramelise and roast off so that their flavours permeate when you add the chestnuts and then the stock.

The trick to obtaining a good stock or soup is to simmer it slowly so that the liquid is consumed gently and has time to absorb all the flavours from your precious ingredients. Season early and make sure your *soffritto* or base is nicely done.

Decent stock always helps a soup, but you can just use water. The soup may not have quite as much depth of flavour, but if you're pressed for time or don't have stock at hand, using water will still work. In the 'Essentials' chapter, I've included methods of preparing good stock. Don't try making tiny batches of stock – it is not worth it for the effort. Make more and freeze what you do not need. That way, you'll always have some delightful homemade stock on hand, fresh as the day you made it. It's so handy, especially for something like *stracciatella*, which is a great restorative after a hard day or when you're not feeling your best. With chicken stock in your freezer, it takes 5 minutes to prepare – pop it in the pot, break the egg, and it's done. I guarantee you'll feel a lot better for it.

*This soup is virtually a meal in itself. I like to use Italian Castelluccio lentils, which have a firm texture and a good flavour, but a cheaper, local lentil will be just as delicious. You will notice the soup darken in colour as it cooks.*

2–3 fennel and pork sausages
  (see Note)
¼ cup olive oil
1 onion, finely chopped
2 cloves garlic, finely chopped
¼ cup speck *or* pancetta,
  cut into small batons
1 carrot, finely chopped
1 stalk celery, finely chopped
375 g lentils
1 tablespoon tomato paste
1 potato, roughly cubed
pinch of salt
pinch of freshly ground black pepper
2 litres Chicken Stock
  (see page 20)
3 bay leaves
1 teaspoon freshly chopped sage
1 teaspoon freshly chopped
  flat-leaf parsley

# Zuppa di lenticchie con salsiccie

## LENTIL SOUP WITH PORK SAUSAGE

Prick the sausages with a fork. Bring a medium pot of water to the boil, then blanch the sausages for 5 minutes. Drain and allow to cool, then slice on the diagonal and set aside.

Heat the olive oil in a large, heavy-based saucepan. To make your *soffritto*, sauté the onion, garlic and speck over a medium heat for 4 minutes, then add the carrot and celery. When the speck begins to colour, add the lentils. Add the tomato paste and stir for 3–4 minutes or until the tomato paste starts to colour a little. Stir in the potato and sausage and season with the salt and pepper. Pour in the stock and add the herbs. Adjust the heat and simmer slowly for about 45 minutes or until the lentils are cooked.   *Serves 8*

Note: There is a huge variety of Italian sausages available. For this style of dish I like to use a more rustic sausage such as *salsiccie*, preferably made by my butcher. If you cultivate a good relationship with your butcher, you should be able to have some input into the flavour of their sausages!

*This really light spring soup is an explosion of fresh herb flavour and the perfect partner to ricotta ravioli. The flavour of the soup is subtle yet distinctive, and feels just right for warmer weather. To me, tasting the soup is like taking a wander through a herb garden. It can also be used with other pasta, or can even be served on its own.*

# Zuppa di erbe con ravioli

## HERB SOUP WITH RICOTTA RAVIOLI

1 bunch spinach
1 tablespoon freshly chopped flat-leaf parsley
1 tablespoon freshly chopped basil
1 tablespoon freshly chopped sage
1 tablespoon freshly chopped marjoram
3 egg yolks
50 ml olive oil
70 g butter
3 tablespoons flour
1 litre cold Chicken *or* Vegetable Stock (*see* page 20)
freshly ground black pepper

*Ricotta ravioli*
250 g fresh ricotta
½ cup freshly grated Parmigiano-Reggiano
sea salt
freshly ground black pepper
freshly grated nutmeg (optional)
500 g Fresh Pasta Dough (*see* page 21)

To make the ricotta ravioli, mix the ricotta with the Parmigiano-Reggiano. Season to taste with salt, pepper and a grating of nutmeg (if using). Roll out the pasta very thinly into 4 sheets, 10 cm × 40 cm. Lay the sheets on your workbench and cut out circles 8 cm in diameter. Lightly brush the edge of half of each circle with water, then put a teaspoon of ricotta filling in the middle. Fold the other half of the circle over the filling and press the edges firmly to seal. Set aside.

Pick the leaves from the spinach and wash them thoroughly 3 times. Bring a large pot of salted water to the boil and blanch the spinach leaves for 2 minutes. Drain and refresh under cold water, then squeeze out the excess water. Using an electric blender, purée the spinach, herbs, egg yolks and olive oil until very smooth. If you wish, pass the mixture through a fine sieve after blending.

Melt the butter in a heavy-based saucepan. Add the flour and mix well with a wooden spoon. Cook for 3–4 minutes, then add the stock, season with pepper and stir continuously until the soup comes to the boil and thickens. Reduce the heat and cook for 5 minutes, mixing thoroughly. Strain the soup into a bowl, then return it to the saucepan and bring back to simmering point (do not boil). Remove from the heat and add the herb purée. Keep warm while you cook the ravioli.

Bring a large pot of salted water to the boil and add the ravioli. Cook for 3 minutes, then lift from the water with a slotted spoon. To serve, put 2 ravioli in each bowl and pour the soup over.   *Serves 6*

*This is a Tuscan classic from the Renaissance period. The cinnamon and vinegar set it apart from other onion soup recipes. This is Italian onion soup – we all know who had it first!*

# Carabaccia

## TUSCAN ONION SOUP

olive oil
10 large onions, sliced
2 cloves garlic, chopped
100 ml red-wine vinegar
1 tablespoon sugar
2 teaspoons ground cinnamon
2.5 litres Chicken Stock
(*see* page 20)
500 g slivered almonds, toasted

Heat ¼ cup olive oil in a large, heavy-based saucepan, then sauté the onion and garlic for 5–8 minutes or until the onion is translucent. Add the vinegar, sugar, cinnamon and stock. Simmer, uncovered, for 45 minutes–1 hour, stirring from time to time to make sure it doesn't stick. Serve immediately, scattered with the almonds and drizzled with olive oil. Offer toasted Italian-style bread to go with the soup.   *Serves 4–6*

*This Roman classic is one of the simplest of all soups, using ingredients that most of us always have on hand – but it is no less satisfying than soups that take more effort to make. It can be garnished with elderflowers.*

# Stracciatella

1 litre Chicken Stock
(*see* page 20)
3 medium eggs
100 g freshly grated Parmigiano-Reggiano
3 pinches freshly chopped flat-leaf parsley
sea salt
freshly ground black pepper
1–2 gratings of fresh nutmeg

Pour the chicken stock into a large pot and bring to boiling point. In a bowl, whisk the eggs, cheese and parsley. Season to taste with salt, pepper and nutmeg and quickly add to the stock. The egg will cook almost instantly. Lightly stir the cooked egg with a fork so that it separates into uneven strands. Serve immediately.   *Serves 4*

Note: *Straccio* means 'in rags', and in this dish the egg looks like strips of cloth floating in a pool of liquid – thus the name *stracciatella*. It is important to let the egg set before breaking it up, otherwise the strands may be too small and the soup will look grainy.

*Opposite: Carabaccia*

*A* minestra *is a soup in which the various ingredients, such as vegetables, pasta and rice, are distinct from the stock in which they are cooked. By contrast, a* zuppa *is thicker and more homogenous. This particular rich, satisfying Tuscan-style* minestra *uses borlotti beans as its base and farro as the garnish. Farro or spelt is an ancient type of wheat. We make much of our bread at the restaurant with spelt flour. The grains are tasty and have great texture, and can be used in much the same way as rice grains – even cooked like a risotto.*

# Minestra di farro

## SPELT SOUP WITH BEANS

400 g borlotti beans, soaked overnight
sea salt
extra-virgin olive oil
1 small white onion, finely chopped
2 cloves garlic, peeled and slightly bruised
1 carrot, finely sliced
1 stick celery, peeled and finely chopped
100 g finely chopped pancetta
3 Roma tomatoes, chopped
2 small potatoes, peeled and chopped
1 tablespoon freshly chopped sage
freshly ground black pepper
½ cup freshly chopped flat-leaf parsley
100 g farro (*see* Note)
freshly grated Parmigiano-Reggiano *or* pecorino

Drain the beans and rinse under cold water. Put into a large saucepan and cover with cold water. Add a little salt. Bring to the boil, then reduce heat to a simmer. Cook, uncovered, for 20 minutes or until just tender. Purée half the beans in a blender with some of the cooking liquid, then set aside. Reserve the remaining beans and cooking liquid.

Heat ½ cup oil in a saucepan and add the onion, garlic, carrot, celery and pancetta. Sauté for 3 minutes, then add the tomato, potato and sage and cook over a medium heat for 2 minutes. Season with salt and pepper.

Add the bean purée and parsley, then stir in the reserved cooking liquid from the beans and simmer for 20 minutes. Add the reserved beans and the farro and cook for a further 20 minutes, adding more water if necessary. Serve drizzled with extra-virgin olive oil and offer Parmigiano-Reggiano at the table.   *Serves 4*

Note: Farro is available at good delicatessens and Italian food stores. If you cannot obtain it, barley can be substituted.

*This winter dish that heralds the season combines the full, rich flavours of forest mushrooms and chestnuts. I like to use mixed dried mushrooms – their wonderful flavours are intensified by the drying process. The soup may be served with the mushroom pieces as they are, or it can be puréed.*

# Zuppa di castagne arrosto e funghi

## ROASTED CHESTNUT AND MUSHROOM SOUP

1 kg chestnuts
50 ml olive oil
1 onion, chopped
2 cloves garlic, chopped
1 bay leaf
200 g dried wild mushrooms, soaked overnight
250 g fresh wild mushrooms (optional), roughly chopped
2 litres Chicken Stock (*see* page 20)
salt
freshly ground black pepper
cream (optional)

Preheat oven to 180°C. Score the bottoms of the chestnuts with a cross and roast for 10–15 minutes until the skin peels back. When the nuts are cool enough to handle, peel them and set aside.

Heat the olive oil in a large, heavy-based pot. Sauté the onion, garlic and bay leaf over a medium heat for 3 minutes, or until the onion is golden. Lift the mushrooms from their soaking liquid (reserve the liquid) and add to the pot. Add the fresh mushrooms at this stage, if using. Add the chestnuts. Cook over a low heat for about 5 minutes, then add the chicken stock and season to taste with salt and pepper. Add a little of the reserved mushroom-soaking water. Simmer gently, uncovered, for about 45 minutes.

Serve immediately if you want a chunky soup. For a smoother soup, transfer it to a food processor and purée until the consistency is to your liking and add a little cream, if you like. Reheat the soup, if necessary, and serve.   *Serves 4–6*

# The Main Event

Sitting down at a dining table evokes a special sense of occasion, and more than a little drama, depending on the gravity of the event. It can be dinner with a couple of friends or with family, or just you and your favourite loved one.

The meal you share can become a celebration, whether you sit down with a piece of bread and a bowl of olive oil, or whether you've gone to a lot of trouble to cook several courses. It may not be a special occasion, like a birthday celebration, but I think every time you sit down to eat together is special.

Dining with people is one of my favourite pastimes, providing the opportunity to catch up, share experiences and create new memories. It's wonderful to remember a particular occasion because of a dish, a flavour or a smell. You eat something and think, *I remember the time when we were down in Sorrento*, or in that restaurant in London or Milan. Or *This reminds me of when we were at the market and we ate on the street*. It will give you cause to celebrate more, because you're remembering happy times that made you feel good. And that's what life's all about it, really, isn't it? Feeling good through the people you love, and the food you eat, and your memories.

Keeping it simple is important, and, even if the dining is to be more formal, great results can be achieved without making the cooking unnecessarily complicated. The event might be grand, but that doesn't necessarily mean you want to be stuck in the kitchen all day. Otherwise, you defeat the purpose of the whole occasion. I know some people get carried away and everything ends up a huge mess, with lots of cleaning up to do. But you can keep it simple with a bit of planning. That's what this section is all about: sitting down and experiencing a meal with people. The meal might be informal, or something you want to dress up a bit. If you're having a lengthy menu, keeping the first course light is a good idea, especially if there's a heavier meat course to follow. Italians always eat pasta as an entrée to a main course, so you might pick a wonderful pasta or soup from 'The Prince and the Pauper'. Or you might prefer some antipasto or a first course from 'Cool Food'. I have included some tasty side dishes here to round off the package.

These main courses are definitely designed to be served on individual plates rather than on platters for sharing. You *could* serve braised oxtail with parsnips (*see* page 94) in a big bowl and have people standing around to eat it, but you'd have a hell of a mess on your hands. It's the sort of dish for which you need to sit down with a knife and fork – and perhaps a bib – and get stuck right into it. *Bollito misto*, the mix of boiled meats (page 97), is the same – there are bits in there that you need to negotiate.

I always end up with a lot left over when I do dinners at home. But leftovers can be great. Obviously they're a great way of quickly coming up with something the next day. As long as you're a bit savvy, and they're stored properly, you can convert leftovers and make a lovely dinner or lunch. In a good Italian kitchen nothing is thrown away. Left over polenta from dinner, for example, is put into a container and refrigerated, so next day it can be made for lunch. Pan fried with a bit of butter or olive oil, it's magnificent with maybe a bit of left over ragout as well. As children we even used to eat left over polenta for breakfast. Mum would simply pan fry it in the morning, we'd eat it and off we'd go.

If there's some left over *bollito misto*, with its wonderful broth, you might strip the meat off and put it back into the broth to make a fantastic soup. With the addition of a bit of rice or pasta, you can make it more substantial. Thinking about your ingredients like this, and modifying them, means you can utilise leftovers very well. Another good example is *riso al salto*, a pan-fried dish made from left over risotto. The next day it can be all pressed into a frying pan, like a big rice cake, and fried until golden on both sides and steamy and warm on the inside. You can cut out slices and it's delicious.

Best of all, some dishes taste better and richer the next day because the flavours have had more time to mix through. Italians call this wonderful intermingling of flavours *intingolo*. A minestrone or a casserole, for example, can be delicious on the day it is made, but the next day is even richer and fuller of flavour. It's had that extra time to sit there, and by warming it up again you've cooked it a bit more and some more liquid has reduced out of it and all the flavours have intensified.

# Hot First Courses

I've included some of my favourites here, including lots of vegetables and seafood, which I find better for starters than richer meat or game dishes. The *cozze alla siciliana* (see page 92) is a great one – a beautifully simple dish of mussels braised in tomato, chilli and olives. Nothing could be easier, and it tastes so real and natural. Just a few mussels served in a big bowl with a spoon so you can get out the juices, with some olives mixed in and some crusty bread or bruschetta, is a magnificent starter before a more robust main course such as a reef fish or oven-roasted barramundi.

*Asparagus is one of those ingredients that marks the season – in this case, spring. I choose larger, fatter spears as they are more fleshy and tender than the fine ones. This recipe incorporates the pungent fontina cheese of Piemonte with delicate, finely cured prosciutto. They're a natural together.*

# Asparagi con prosciutto, fontina e uovo in camicia

## ASPARAGUS WITH PROSCIUTTO, FONTINA AND POACHED EGG

24 asparagus spears, trimmed
200 g fontina cheese, thinly sliced
100 ml cream
salt
freshly ground black pepper
1½ tablespoons white vinegar
4 large free-range eggs
8 slices prosciutto
2 handfuls watercress

Preheat the griller to hot. Bring a large pot of salted water to the boil. Add the asparagus and blanch for 12 minutes, then drain and transfer to a baking tray. Cover with the slices of fontina and pour the cream over as evenly as possible. Season with salt and pepper. Grill for 5–10 minutes until the cheese has melted. Remove from the heat and keep warm.

Meanwhile, fill a shallow pan with water and add the vinegar. Bring to the boil, then reduce the heat to just below simmering (95°C). Using a slotted spoon, swirl the water around, then, while the water is moving, add 1 egg. Poach for 3–4 minutes – the yolk should still be runny. Lift the egg out with a slotted spoon and drain. Keep warm while you poach the remaining eggs.

Serve each diner with 5–6 asparagus spears. Top with 2 slices prosciutto and then a poached egg. Drizzle with any juices from the baking tray, scatter with watercress and serve.   *Serves 4*

*Roasting whole scallops in their shell rather than on the half-shell makes this dish richer and the flavour more intense. Leeks are a superb accompaniment to scallops, so here I have paired them with little soufflés, which are also great as a vegetarian option without the scallops.*

# Cape sante vive con soffiato di porri

## LIVE GIANT TASMANIAN SCALLOPS WITH LEEK SOUFFLÉS

250 g softened butter
1 clove garlic, crushed
1 teaspoon freshly grated lemon zest
1 teaspoon freshly chopped basil
1 teaspoon freshly chopped coriander
1 teaspoon freshly chopped flat-leaf parsley
freshly chopped chilli (to taste)
sea salt
freshly ground black pepper
24 live Spring Bay or similar scallops (see Note), cleaned

### Leek soufflés
olive oil
1 leek, finely sliced and washed
350 ml milk
60 g butter
60 g flour
75 g gruyère cheese
4 eggs, separated

To make the soufflés, lightly grease 8 small moulds with olive oil and preheat the oven to 180°C. Heat 1½ tablespoons olive oil in a frying pan, then add the leek and sauté gently for about 10 minutes, tossing until soft. Transfer the leek to a food processor and blend until not quite smooth. Set aside. Gently bring the milk to a boil in a heavy-based saucepan. Meanwhile, melt the butter in another heavy-based saucepan, then add the flour and stir with a wooden spoon to combine. Add the hot milk and stir continuously until blended. Reduce the heat and cook for 5–10 minutes, stirring continuously, until thick. Add the cheese and the leek purée. Stir to combine, then remove the saucepan from the heat and allow to cool to room temperature or a little warmer. Add the egg yolks one at a time, incorporating each yolk before adding the next one. Whisk the egg whites until fluffy, then fold into the yolk mixture. Spoon the mixture into the prepared moulds and put them into a baking tray. Pour in cold water to reach three-quarters up the sides of the moulds, then cover the tray with aluminium foil. Bake for 25 minutes.

    Meanwhile, put the butter, garlic, lemon zest, herbs and chilli into the bowl of an electric mixer fitted with a paddle beater. Season to taste with salt and pepper. Beat for 3–4 minutes until well combined. Using a small, sharp knife, pry open each scallop just enough to insert a tablespoon of the butter mixture. Arrange the filled scallops on a baking tray and put into the oven with the soufflés. Bake for 5 minutes or until the scallops open and the butter is sizzling, and the souffles are puffed up and golden brown on top. Serve immediately, with 2–3 scallops per person.   *Serves 8*

Note: Live scallops are sold in their complete shell. Spring Bay scallops, which are farmed in very cold water and are pure and clean, are becoming more readily available at good fishmongers. Any high-quality fresh scallops in the shell can be used for this dish.

olive oil
6 large quail (see Note)
6 handfuls rocket leaves

*Marinade*
50 ml olive oil
100 ml verjuice
50 ml vincotto (see page 40)
2½ tablespoons honey
1 clove garlic, chopped
1 small chilli, seeded and chopped
juice and grated zest of 2 limes
leaves from 4 sprigs rosemary
sea salt
freshly ground black pepper

*Mushroom broth*
50 g mixed dried mushrooms, soaked overnight
50 g shiitake mushrooms
50 g Swiss brown mushrooms
50 g pine forest mushrooms
50 ml olive oil
1 small onion, diced
1 clove garlic, chopped
1 medium carrot, diced
1 stick celery, diced
1 large potato, diced
sea salt
freshly ground black pepper
1 litre Chicken Stock (see page 20)
1 bay leaf
1 teaspoon freshly chopped sage
½ cup freshly chopped flat-leaf parsley
1 teaspoon crushed fresh basil

*Mushrooms taste so good in autumn. I know you can get many types of fungi all year round, but the taste of them in season, especially in a broth like this one, is the best.*

# Quaglie arrosto con brodo di funghi

## ROASTED QUAIL WITH MUSHROOM BROTH

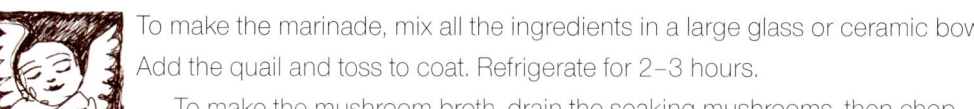

To make the marinade, mix all the ingredients in a large glass or ceramic bowl. Add the quail and toss to coat. Refrigerate for 2–3 hours.

To make the mushroom broth, drain the soaking mushrooms, then chop roughly. Chop the other mushrooms roughly. Set all the chopped mushrooms aside. Heat the olive oil in a large, heavy-based saucepan. Add the onion and garlic and sauté over a medium heat for about 3 minutes or until translucent. Add the carrot and celery and sauté for 3 minutes, stirring occasionally. Add the mushrooms and potato and season with salt and pepper. Stir well. Pour in the stock and mix well. Add the bay leaf, sage, parsley and basil. Reduce the heat and simmer, uncovered, for 30 minutes.

Preheat the oven to 180°C. Heat a baking tray on the stove, then add a little olive oil. Seal the quail for 1 minute on each side, then transfer the tray to the oven and bake for 10 minutes. Remove from the oven and allow to rest for a couple of minutes, then transfer the quail to a chopping board. Using a large, heavy knife, cut each quail in half lengthwise by inserting the knife into the cavity, then cutting through the backbone, then turning the quail over and cutting through the breast bone.

Serve each person with 2 quail halves. Ladle over the mushroom broth and scatter with rocket leaves.    *Serves 6*

Note: Quail is a delicate game bird and a great introduction for people who haven't tried game birds before. They are commonly available from good poultry stores or butchers.

*Nothing could be easier than this beautiful, simple dish of mussels braised in tomato, chilli and olives. It can be a soup, a pasta sauce or a hearty meal in itself. The liquid becomes powerfully flavoursome because of the natural juices imparted from the mussels.*

200 ml olive oil
1 onion, diced
1 clove garlic, thinly sliced
1 stick celery, finely chopped
2 tablespoons tomato paste
freshly chopped chilli (to taste)
handful of basil leaves
½ cup freshly chopped
   flat-leaf parsley
pinch of dried *or* freshly chopped
   oregano
1 × 400 g can crushed tomatoes
200 ml white wine
1 kg mussels in the shell
   (*see* Note), cleaned
sea salt
freshly ground black pepper
200 g olives, pitted

# Cozze alla siciliana

## BRAISED MUSSELS WITH TOMATO, CHILLI AND OLIVES

Heat the olive oil in a heavy-based saucepan. Sauté the onion until translucent, then add the garlic and celery and cook until the celery is soft. Add the tomato paste, chilli and herbs and cook until the tomato paste deepens in colour (caramelises). Stir in the tomatoes and wine and simmer gently, uncovered, for 15 minutes.

Add the mussels, then season with salt and pepper and put on the lid. Leave for about 5 minutes, then lift the lid carefully to see whether the mussels have opened. If necessary, mix the mussels gently and cook, covered, for a little longer. Add the olives and serve immediately.  *Serves 4*

Note: Use the freshest mussels you can find – if they aren't quite fresh, you will taste that lack of freshness through the whole dish. I like to use local mussels when the season is good, but also recommend Tasmanian Spring Bay mussels, which are plump and meaty.

# Meat and Game

I have always been known as a meaty bloke, so it's no surprise main-course meat dishes are my favourite part of the menu. I love all those rich casseroles and braised dishes, not to mention the roasts of larger cuts of meat that come out tender and juicy from the oven and fill the kitchen with wicked aromas. Many things can be added to meat to change the direction of flavour – I'm always using different herbs, vegetables and spices.

Different meat cuts require different treatments and applications, which means it is important to choose the correct cut for the recipe you are planning to cook. For example, long braising is not the right method for cooking a fillet of beef; similarly, quick grilling is unsuitable for an ox cheek. The ageing process is also an important part of any meat's make-up. It is a good idea to talk to your butcher to get a clue as to the age of the meat you plan to buy, and how this might affect its cooking.

One of my favourite meat dishes is *bollito misto* (*see* page 97). It's a dish of mixed boiled meats, which might include a bit of tongue, a bit of the Italian sausage *cotechino*, maybe some beef, and some chicken. Some people turn up their nose at boiled meat, but it can be the tastiest thing in the world. 'Boiled' is probably a bit harsh to describe it – the meats are really gently poached. Once all the meats are cooked in there, you have a beautiful broth.

Roasting game birds is a dangerous practice for me, too, as their sweet, succulent, gamey flesh always proves a temptation. There's nothing quite like a good bird!

*My dad taught me to cook oxtail, one of the richest of all meats. If you are new to oxtail, you will be delighted to discover its incredible depth of flavour. Sometimes I use it to make soup or stock – it's just brilliant. Cook it long and slow, and the meat should come away from the bone with ease. It is quite lush, quite Roman, when cooked according to this recipe. I like it served with mashed potato or parsnip.*

# Coda di bue brasata con vino rosso

## BRAISED OXTAIL WITH TOMATO AND RED WINE AND BRAISED PARSNIP

2 kg oxtail (*see* Note)
olive oil
1 medium onion, chopped
1 clove garlic, chopped
2 carrots, chopped
1 stick celery, chopped
2 bay leaves
1 sprig thyme
¼ cup freshly chopped flat-leaf parsley
6 cloves
½ teaspoon freshly grated nutmeg
sea salt
freshly ground black pepper
⅔ cup tomato paste
¾ cup red wine
500 ml Beef Stock (*see* page 19)

*Braised parsnip*
50 ml olive oil
½ medium onion, chopped
4 medium parsnips, peeled and roughly sliced
45 ml Chicken Stock (*see* page 20)
50 ml cream
sea salt
freshly ground black pepper

Preheat the oven to 200°C. Put the oxtail on a baking tray and drizzle with olive oil. Roast for 20 minutes, turning to allow the meat to brown evenly.

Heat 2 tablespoons olive oil in a large, heavy-based pot. Add the onion and garlic and sauté over a medium heat until the garlic is almost golden. Add the carrot, celery, herbs and spices and season to taste, then cook gently without allowing the vegetables to brown. Add the tomato paste and cook, stirring continuously, until the tomato paste deepens in colour (caramelises). Add the oxtail, then pour in enough wine and stock to cover. Simmer for 1 hour, uncovered, or until the liquid has reduced to a thick sauce and the meat is tender.

Meanwhile, make the braised parsnip. Heat the oil in a pot, then add the onion and sauté over a high heat for 2–3 minutes until translucent but not coloured. Add the parsnip and sauté for 2–3 minutes. Add the stock and cream and bring to the boil. Reduce the heat and simmer, uncovered, for 20 minutes until the parsnips are tender and most of the liquid has evaporated. Season to taste with salt and pepper.

To serve, ladle the oxtail, vegetables and sauce into deep plates. Spoon the parsnip into separate bowls.   *Serves 4–6*

Note: You need larger, more robust oxtails for this dish. Give your butcher plenty of notice so as to ensure the best-quality meat is available.

*Bollito misto basically translates as 'mixed boiled'. People might think this is a simple dish to make – after all, how difficult can it be to boil some meat? The fact is that the true mastery of cookery is shown in many aspects of the dish, and a great deal of care and pride must be taken to obtain an excellent result. With several hours' preparation and cooking time required, it is a test of patience as well as devotion. But the result is layers of flavours that can only be obtained by slow cooking. In the Veneto they love to serve boiled meats with piera. Try it with mustard fruits, too.*

# Bollito misto con piera

## BOILED MEATS WITH PIERA

2 fresh chicken carcasses
1 ox cheek, trimmed
    and well rinsed (*see* Note)
2 onions, chopped
2 carrots, chopped
2 sticks celery, chopped
½ cup freshly chopped
    flat-leaf parsley
3 bay leaves
sea salt
freshly ground black pepper
1 pickled ox tongue (*see* Note)
1 high-quality cotechino sausage
1 loaf stale bread, crust removed
1 litre milk
4 chicken Marylands
½ clove garlic, chopped
large handful of freshly grated
    Parmigiano-Reggiano
1 egg
1 kg minced beef
12 egg whites
6 Spunta potatoes
    (*or* other variety)
8 baby carrots, peeled
1–2 litres Chicken Stock
    (*see* page 20)
250 g cavolo nero (*see* Note)
1 kg fresh broad beans, shelled

Put the chicken carcasses and ox cheek into a medium-sized pot. Add half the onion, half the carrot, half the celery, half the parsley, the bay leaves and a pinch of salt and pepper. Cover generously with water and bring to the boil. Reduce the heat and simmer for about 1 hour, skimming from time to time to remove any impurities.

Meanwhile, put the tongue and *cotechino* into a separate pot. Add the remaining onion, carrot and celery, half the remaining parsley, and a pinch of salt and pepper. Cover with plenty of water and bring to the boil. Reduce the heat and simmer for about 1 hour, skimming from time to time to remove any impurities. Remove the pot from the heat and set aside.

Tear the bread into pieces, then soak in the milk for 10 minutes. Meanwhile, lay each chicken Maryland skin-side down on your work surface. Gently cut along the leg bone until the bone is exposed, then insert the knife under the bone and cut the flesh away, leaving the leg bone free and flat.

Squeeze most of the milk out of the bread – it needs to remain moist. Transfer the bread to an electric blender and add the garlic and a pinch of salt and pepper. Add the Parmigiano-Reggiano, the remaining parsley and the egg and blend well until the mixture is firm but not too dry or too wet (if it is too runny, add some dried breadcrumbs). Spoon some filling into each chicken Maryland, then roll it into a sausage shape and tie securely with kitchen string.

Transfer the chicken Marylands to the pot with the ox cheek, then simmer for about 20 minutes or until the chicken is cooked through and feels firm to the touch. Remove the chicken and set aside. Simmer the stock for a further 30 minutes – the total cooking time for the stock should be 2 hours. Remove the ox cheek, which should be very tender but still intact, and set aside. Strain the stock and allow it to cool completely. ▶

*Piera*
1 litre Chicken Stock
   (*see* page 20)
1 cup fine dried breadcrumbs
a little freshly grated
   Parmigiano-Reggiano
a drizzle of olive oil
freshly ground white pepper

Put the cold stock into a clean pot and add the minced beef and egg whites. Mix well. Cook over an extremely low heat, stirring often, until the egg whites start to coagulate. At this point a 'raft' of egg whites and mince will form over the stock, allowing the stock to clarify. Using a wooden spoon, gently make a hole in the raft so that the spoon can be put through to move any sediment at the bottom of the pot and prevent it from burning. Simmer gently for 1 hour, stirring the sediment occasionally. Remove from the heat and discard the 'raft'. Strain the stock very carefully and slowly through a strainer lined with muslin into a clean container. Set aside the clarified stock or consommé, which will be golden and delightfully clear.

Meanwhile, peel the potatoes and cut them into golfball-sized pieces. Put into a saucepan with the baby carrots and pour in enough chicken stock to cover. Bring to the boil, then cook for 15–20 minutes or until tender. Drain and keep warm. Remove and discard the central stem from the *cavolo nero* leaves and wash the leaves well. Wipe out the saucepan, then pour in 2 cups stock and bring to the boil. Blanch the *cavolo nero* for 3 minutes. Drain and keep warm.

Bring a separate large pot of salted water to the boil and add the broad beans. When the water returns to the boil, drain the beans and refresh quickly in cold water. Remove and discard the husks or second skins from the beans. Set the beans aside.

To make the *piera*, bring the stock to a boil and stir in the breadcrumbs. Add the Parmigiano-Reggiano and olive oil and as much white pepper as you can handle. Cook for a few minutes, then set aside and keep warm.

Put the chicken Marylands and the ox cheek into a pot and ladle over a little consommé. Gently bring to the boil. Warm up the other meats in their own stock. Gently warm the remaining consommé.

To serve, arrange the potatoes, baby carrots and *cavolo nero* in deep plates with a smattering of broad beans. Slice all the cooked meats and arrange with the vegetables. Ladle on a generous amount of the consommé.   *Serves 8*

Note: Ox cheek and pickled ox tongue are available at good butchers. *Cavolo nero* is from the kale family and is also known as Tuscan cabbage. It is traditionally used in soups such as *ribollita*, but I like to serve it as a stand-alone vegetable dish as well, simply blanched in salted boiling water and dressed with olive oil, salt, pepper and a squeeze of lemon juice. The young leaves can be quickly sautéed and added to many different dishes to provide a refreshing crunch.

*These little lamb chops are just so quick and easy. Scotta ditto means 'to burn the fingers', and that's what happens if you grab these tasty morsels too soon after they are cooked. The olive paste adds a delicious layer of flavour.*

# Scotta ditto all'olivo

## LAMB CHOPS WITH ALMOND AND OLIVE

2½ tablespoons black olive paste (*see* Note)
50 g ground almonds
1 clove garlic, chopped
1 teaspoon freshly chopped rosemary leaves
sea salt
freshly ground black pepper
12 lamb loin chops
olive oil

Using a mortar and pestle, pound the olive paste, ground almonds, garlic and rosemary to a paste. Add salt and pepper to taste.

Using a meat mallet, lightly pound the lamb chops to flatten them slightly. Put them into a glass or ceramic dish, then brush each one with some olive-and-almond mixture. Using your fingers, massage the paste into the meat on both sides until the chops are well covered. Cover the dish with plastic wrap and refrigerate for 30 minutes.

Preheat the griller or a chargrill pan to hot. Add a little oil, then sear the chops for 2–3 minutes on each side. They should be crispy on the outside and pink in the middle. Serve immediately with fried potatoes (see page 120).   *Serves 4*

Note: While it is possible to buy ready-made olive paste, I like to make my own. Simply blend your favourite pitted black olives with a little olive oil.

*When my daughter, Loredana, had her first communion I wanted to serve something festive that everybody would love. Duck is one of her favourites, and who doesn't like a bit of pie? So, with the addition of some spices and with a little* vincotto *(see page 40) providing some sweetness, I had my crowd-pleaser well under way. This pie looks fantastic at the table.*

# Torta di anatra

## DUCK PIE

1 onion, finely chopped
1 stick celery, finely chopped
1 clove garlic, chopped
1 × 2 kg duck
1 teaspoon juniper berries, crushed
1 tablespoon freshly chopped rosemary
sea salt
freshly ground black pepper
300 ml white wine
100 g cavolo nero
50 ml vincotto
100 ml verjuice
500 g Shortcrust Pastry (see page 23)
500 g Puff Pastry (see page 22)
1 egg
milk

Preheat the oven to 180°C. Scatter the onion, celery and garlic in a roasting tray, then put the duck on top of the vegetables. Add the juniper berries and rosemary and season to taste with salt and pepper. Pour in the white wine. Roast for 30 minutes, basting from time to time. If the wine evaporates, add a little more as necessary. Remove the tray from the oven and set the duck aside until it is cool enough to handle. Leave the oven on.

Remove and discard the central stems from the *cavolo nero* and wash the leaves well. Pull the duck meat from the carcass and return the meat to the roasting tray. (Discard the carcass, or reserve it for making stock.) Add the *vincotto* and verjuice and cook over a moderate heat for 3–4 minutes, stirring continuously. Add the *cavolo nero* and cook for 3–4 minutes until the leaves have wilted, stirring to prevent sticking. Remove the tray from the heat and set aside.

Roll out the shortcrust pastry to a thickness of about 3 mm, then line a 12 cm diameter, 5 cm deep pie dish with it. Allow to rest for 20 minutes.

Transfer the contents of the roasting tray to the pie dish. Roll out the puff pastry to a thickness of about 3 mm. Whisk the egg with a little milk, then brush the edges of the shortcrust pastry with some of the egg mixture. Lay the puff pastry over the pie. Pinch the edges and cut off any excess pastry, ensuring that it seals well. Brush the top of the pie with the remaining egg mixture and cut a small hole in the centre of the lid to allow steam to escape. Bake for 35 minutes or until golden brown. Remove from the oven and serve hot.

Note: Making your own pastry can be time-consuming, but it is great fun and very rewarding. If time is an issue for you, ask your local pastry shop to make some for you. Any leftover pastry should be wrapped and kept for another use. It freezes really well.

*I love to cook birds like these pheasants at home. There's no need to embellish the dish unnecessarily; its natural, earthy flavours will come to the fore naturally.*

1 onion, diced
1 medium carrot, sliced
1 stick celery, chopped
2 × 1 kg pheasants (see Note)
100 ml olive oil
1 clove garlic, chopped
1 star anise, crushed
sea salt
freshly ground black pepper
2 sprigs rosemary
1 teaspoon freshly chopped sage
2 bay leaves
300 ml white wine
300 ml Chicken Stock
   (see page 20)

### Porcini sauce
50 ml olive oil
1 small onion, chopped
1 clove garlic
100 g porcini mushrooms,
   soaked for at least 1 hour
200 ml white wine
500 ml Demi-glace (see page 19)
sea salt
freshly ground black pepper

# Fagiano con porcini

## PHEASANT WITH PORCINI SAUCE

Preheat the oven to 180°C. Scatter the vegetables in a large roasting tray. Rub the skin of the birds with the olive oil and sprinkle with the garlic, star anise, salt and pepper. Put the seasoned birds on top of the vegetables in the tray. Add the rosemary, sage, bay leaves, wine and stock and roast for 30–40 minutes, basting from time to time.

    Meanwhile, make the porcini sauce. Heat the olive oil in a heavy-based pot, then add the onion and garlic and sauté for 3–4 minutes until golden brown. Lift the porcini from their soaking water and add them to the pot. Sauté for 2–3 minutes, then add the white wine and demi-glace. Reduce the heat and simmer for 20 minutes. Season to taste with salt and pepper.

    To serve, transfer the pheasants to a platter and spoon over some of the porcini sauce. Cut the meat off the bone at the table and offer the remaining sauce in a jug.   *Serves 4–6*

Note: Guinea fowl or even a really good chook can be prepared in this way with exciting results. We can buy great free-range chickens these days, and game birds are more readily available as well. Most markets have good poultry stores that deal in these products.

*Cold weather and shanks – the two seem so natural together. The thought of steam rising from tender flesh that falls from the bone makes me feel warm and snuggly. I use lentils in this version, but beans (perhaps cannellini beans) would be good too. Try it with lamb shanks instead of veal, if you prefer.*

## Stinco di vitello con lenticchie

### BRAISED VEAL SHANKS WITH LENTILS

6 veal shanks
2 litres Chicken Stock (see page 20)
  or Veal Stock (see page 19)
75 ml olive oil
1 small onion, diced
1 clove garlic, finely chopped
1 small carrot, diced
1 stick celery, diced
1 potato, diced
½ cup flour
½ cup good-quality small lentils
sea salt
freshly ground black pepper
2 bay leaves
1 teaspoon freshly chopped sage
½ cup freshly chopped flat-leaf parsley
grated zest of 1 lemon
50 ml cream (optional)

 Preheat the oven to 180°C. Put the shanks into a large, heavy-based pot and pour in the stock. Bring to the boil and cook for 15 minutes. Gently remove the shanks from the liquid and put them into a large baking dish. Strain the cooking liquid and reserve.

Wipe out the pot and heat the olive oil over a moderate heat. Add the onion and garlic and sauté, stirring, for 2 minutes. Add the carrot, celery and potato and sauté for 3–4 minutes. Add the flour and stir continuously for 2 minutes. Pour in the reserved broth and mix together vigorously to prevent the flour forming lumps. Add the lentils, then season to taste with salt and pepper and add the bay leaves, sage, parsley and lemon zest.

Carefully pour the contents of the pot over the shanks and transfer the baking dish to the oven. Braise for 30 minutes or until the lentils are cooked and the veal is tender. If desired, add the cream and gently mix through so as not to break up the shanks. Serve immediately.
*Serves 6*

*Some combinations of flavours are truly special, such as the one featured here: game, red wine and chocolate. Rooted in Piemontese tradition, this preparation can be used for hare, wild boar or any of the richer game meats. Don't use lean cuts, as the cooking will dry the meat. The spices give incredible depth, and the cocoa provides an amazing twist. Cut the meat small enough and you have an opulent ragù for pappardelle.*

# Cervo in salmì

## VENISON STEW

2 kg boned venison shoulder (see Note), cut into cubes
200 ml olive oil
1 cup tomato paste
1 litre veal, chicken or beef stock (see pages 19–20) or venison stock
1 tablespoon Dutch cocoa
1 tablespoon strawberry jam
1 teaspoon brandy

*Marinade*
1 onion, diced
1 large carrot, diced
1 large stick celery, diced
2 cloves garlic, crushed
1 teaspoon freshly chopped rosemary
1 teaspoon freshly chopped sage
1 teaspoon freshly chopped flat-leaf parsley
1 teaspoon juniper berries, crushed
pinch of freshly grated nutmeg
pinch of ground cumin
1 litre red wine
sea salt
freshly ground black pepper

To make the marinade, combine all the ingredients in a large glass or ceramic dish. Add the venison, turning to coat. Cover and refrigerate overnight.

Next day, remove the meat from the marinade. Strain the marinade and reserve both the liquid and the vegetables.

Heat 50 ml of the olive oil in a large, heavy-based pot. Add the venison and brown on all sides. Remove from the pot and set aside. Heat another 50 ml of the olive oil in the pot, then add the reserved vegetables and sauté for 3–4 minutes. Add the tomato paste and cook for 5 minutes, stirring continuously to prevent sticking. Return the venison to the pot and pour in the reserved marinade liquid and the stock. Mix well, then reduce the heat and simmer gently for 1 hour, stirring occasionally to prevent sticking.

Put the cocoa, jam and brandy in a bowl. Heat until the cocoa has dissolved, mixing well to avoid lumps. Add the cocoa mixture to the stew and mix well. Cook for a further 5 minutes, then taste a piece of the meat – it should be tender. Serve immediately, accompanied by polenta (see page 23) if you like.   Serves 6

Note: Venison is deep red in colour and has a distinctive flavour that I find delicious. It is farmed in Australia but can be expensive to purchase, especially prime cuts such as the saddle or back legs. This dish uses the shoulder, which is cheaper to buy and more appropriate for long cooking than other cuts due to its higher proportion of fat. Venison is readily available from specialist meat stores, but can be obtained by most butchers if you give them a bit of notice.

*Classically Venetian, this dish is full of flavour and relies on the skill of using the pan quickly – it must be hot enough but not too hot, and the onions need to caramelise and the liver must sizzle beautifully without burning. Some recipes call for Marsala, but I don't think it's necessary – if the onions are cooked right, they provide sufficient sweetness.*

# Fegato alla veneziana

PAN-FRIED CALF'S LIVER WITH ONIONS AND WHITE WINE

50 ml olive oil
25 g butter
2 large onions, thinly sliced
1 tablespoon freshly chopped sage
1 kg calf's liver, trimmed and very thinly sliced
flour
sea salt
freshly ground black pepper
100 ml dry white wine
½ cup finely chopped flat-leaf parsley

In a frying pan, heat the oil and half the butter until it begins to bubble. Add the onion and sage, then reduce the heat and cook for 5 minutes until softened.

Lightly dust the calf's liver with flour, then add to the pan and brown on both sides – this will take only a few minutes and the liver should still be a little rare in the centre. Season with salt and pepper. Remove the liver from the pan and keep warm. By this time the onion should be lightly coloured.

Deglaze the pan with the white wine, then reduce over a high heat for 3–4 minutes to form a sauce. Return the liver to the pan and add the parsley and the remaining butter, mixing well. Serve immediately.   *Serves 4*

# Fish and Seafood

With so much of Italy surrounded by water, it's no surprise that every region seems to have a fish or seafood speciality. In Tuscany, a town called Livorno has a wonderful dish called *cacciucco*, which is a rich braise of fish and seafood in a tomato fish stock. The word has five Cs, and you're meant to include at least five different fish to make it work.

The Italian love of seafood is easily applied to Australia because of our magnificent diversity of seafood and fish. We've got so much to choose from, and people are eating more and more of it. Nowadays, in the restaurant we can sustain four or five different fish dishes on any one night, whereas once upon a time we'd just have 'the fish'. People understand a lot more about fish these days, too. They know that John Dory is certainly not snapper – it's like comparing a piece of veal to a piece of beef. With people eating more fish, we are able to experiment more in the kitchen.

For this book I've chosen a small selection of beautiful, aromatic fish dishes, such as snapper *al cartoccio* (*see* page 108). The snapper fillets are wrapped in paper and baked, and when you send them to the dining room and open them at the table, the room is instantly filled with a wonderful aroma of the fish and herbs inside the wrapping. It's very appetising. I've also included a shiraz risotto (page 110), which goes well with snapper or coral trout, because the richness of the red wine works so well with the lovely light, clean fish. There's a dish with scampi (page 112), a beautiful seafood popular in the Italian *cucina*. Another one I really love is *calamari ripieni* (page 109). This is a delightful way of presenting calamari, with the whole body stuffed.

As I said in the 'Essentials' chapter, it's important when buying fish to make sure everything is very fresh and in optimum condition. The key is not necessarily buying what you want at the time, but the best available.

*This is a great way of filling the house with aromas. When your guests open the paper at the table, all the wonderful smells from cooking the fish are released.*

# Dentice in cartoccio

## FILLETS OF SNAPPER BAKED IN PAPER

100 g cavolo nero
50 ml olive oil
1 clove garlic, crushed
2 tablespoons freshly crushed ginger
1 stick celery, cut into batons
4 large sprigs flat-leaf parsley
4 large sprigs coriander
200 g freshly picked crab meat (see Note)
sea salt
freshly ground black pepper
8 baby snapper fillets (see Note)
100 g butter, melted

Preheat the oven to 200°C. Remove and discard the central stems from the *cavolo nero* and wash the leaves well. Heat the olive oil in a large frying pan. Briefly sauté the garlic and ginger over a high heat, then add the *cavolo nero*, celery and herbs and sauté until the *cavolo nero* has wilted. Stir in the crab meat and season with salt and pepper. Remove from the heat.

If you wish, 'pin-bone' the snapper fillets – run your finger along the fish to find the tiny bones in the flesh, then, using tweezers, remove them. Cut 8 sheets of greaseproof paper to 3 times the length of the snapper fillets. Lay one of the sheets on your workbench and brush well with melted butter. Put a fish fillet on one end of the paper, skin-side down. Season with a little salt and pepper, then spoon on some crab mixture. Top with a second fillet, skin-side up, to form a 'sandwich'. Draw up the sides of the paper and wrap well. Put the parcel on a baking tray. Repeat with the remaining snapper fillets and crab mixture. Bake for 10 minutes. Serve immediately with fennel and orange salad (see page 51). Let your guests unwrap their parcel at the table to enjoy the wonderful aromas.   Serves 4

Note: Ask your fishmonger for fresh crab meat. They should also stock small fish such as baby snapper, which I use here. However, any moist fillet – or even a whole fish – will do.

*Full of flavour, this is a sensational way of presenting calamari, especially to little ones. It's earthy, yet somehow very elegant, and always reminds me of the Venetian cucina, which is rich in recipes for cephalopods. Allow the dish to cool before serving, and it makes a superb antipasto.*

# Calamari ripieni

## STUFFED CALAMARI

12 baby calamari (see Note), cleaned
100 ml olive oil
2 shallots, finely chopped
1 clove garlic, finely chopped
1 teaspoon freshly grated ginger
1 teaspoon finely chopped coriander leaves
grated zest of 1 lemon
¼ cup freshly chopped flat-leaf parsley
½ cup green peas, blanched
sea salt
freshly ground black pepper
½ cup dried breadcrumbs
100 ml white wine

Leave the calamari bodies intact, but cut the tentacles and wings into small dice. Heat half the olive oil in a large frying pan. Add the shallots and cook gently until translucent but not coloured. Add the garlic, ginger, coriander, lemon zest and two-thirds of the parsley, then add the calamari dice to the pan and cook gently for about 5 minutes. Add the peas and season to taste with salt and pepper. Gently stir in the breadcrumbs, then remove from the heat and allow to cool.

Preheat the oven to 180°C. Fill the calamari bodies with the cooled shallot mixture, securing the end of each tube with a toothpick by weaving it through as if sewing. Heat the remaining olive oil in a large ovenproof dish. Add the stuffed calamari and cook over a medium heat on each side until golden. Pour in the white wine and season with salt and pepper. Put the dish into the oven for 10 minutes or until heated through. To serve, sprinkle with the remaining parsley and spoon over the juices.   *Serves 4*

Note: Baby calamari are not always easy to obtain, but with a bit of notice a good fishmonger should be able to organise them for you. You could use larger calamari, but it is worth the extra effort to use baby calamari (they are a bit fiddly to deal with).

*The whole combination – the fish, the risotto and the sauce – works in harmony here. The red-wine risotto works with meat, too, and can be made into a real feature on its own as a first course.*

# Pesce arrosto con zafferano e risotto al vino rosso

## ROASTED REEF FISH WITH SAFFRON MUSSEL SAUCE AND RED-WINE RISOTTO

100 ml olive oil
1 × 2 kg fillet reef fish (*see* Note), cut into 250 g portions
flour
sea salt
freshly ground black pepper

*Red-wine risotto*
1 tablespoon olive oil
1 onion, finely chopped
1 clove garlic, finely chopped
3 cups arborio rice
sea salt
freshly ground black pepper
1.25 litres Chicken Stock (*see* page 20)
1.25 litres shiraz
50 g butter
1 cup freshly grated Parmigiano-Reggiano

*Saffron mussel sauce*
12 mussels in the shell, cleaned
1 bottle pinot grigio *or* other dry white wine
100 g butter
2 shallots, diced
1 clove garlic, finely chopped
1 small carrot, diced
1 stick celery, diced
1 teaspoon saffron threads
2 cups cream

To make the risotto, heat the oil in a heavy-based saucepan. Add the onions and garlic and gently sauté until translucent. Add the rice and season with salt and pepper. Cook, stirring, for 1–2 minutes, then stir in the stock and wine. Bring to the boil, then reduce heat to medium and simmer for about 20 minutes, stirring occasionally, until the rice has soaked up all the liquid. Add the butter and Parmigiano-Reggiano and stir until creamy. Set aside and keep warm.

To make the sauce, put the mussels into a large pot and pour in half the wine. Cover, then set over a high heat for a few minutes. Lift the lid carefully to see whether the mussels have opened. If they haven't, stir gently, replace the lid and cook for a little longer. Transfer the mussels to a dish. Strain the cooking liquid and set aside. Meanwhile, melt the butter in a deep frying pan and gently sauté the shallots, garlic, carrot and celery for about 5 minutes until soft but not coloured. Add the saffron and cook until slightly toasted and the colour bleeds out. Pour in the strained liquid, then add the cream and the remaining wine. Reduce by half over a low heat. Remove the mussel flesh from the shells and stir it into the sauce.

Preheat the oven to 180°C. Gently heat the olive oil in an ovenproof pan. Lightly dust the fish with flour, then put into the pan skin-side down. Seal well on one side for 2–3 minutes, then turn and seal on the other side. Season with salt and pepper. Transfer the pan to the oven and bake for 12 minutes or until cooked all the way through and firm to the touch.

When ready to serve, gently heat the sauce until warmed through. Arrange 2 pieces of roasted fish on each plate and spoon some risotto next to them. Drizzle the sauce around, allowing 3 mussels per person.  *Serves 4*

Note: A 'reef fish' is one that lives on a coral reef. Any of the larger firm-fleshed fish will do well here. Barramundi is great, as is emperor, or one of my favourites, coral trout. Talk to your fishmonger about what fish is best on the day you shop, and get him or her to portion the fish for you, to save time.

*This recipe illustrates how excellent ingredients can stand on their own without too much tarting up. Great food does not get much easier – but, easy or not, you will be salivating at the thought of this! Prawns and other crustaceans can be done in this way, too.*

## Scampi alla piastra con cetriolo

### GRILLED SCAMPI WITH CUCUMBER SALAD

12 large scampi (see Note)
sea salt
freshly ground black pepper
1 teaspoon freshly chopped chilli
2 tablespoons freshly chopped
    flat-leaf parsley
juice of 1 lemon
½ cup extra-virgin olive oil

*Cucumber salad*
1 long cucumber, diced
200 g sheep's milk yoghurt
1 teaspoon freshly chopped mint
sea salt
freshly ground black pepper

Cut each scampi in half lengthwise by firmly holding it belly-side down on a board, then, using a large, sharp knife, cutting into the head and down through the tail. Transfer to a deep tray, cut side up. Season with salt and pepper, then scatter over the chilli and parsley. Add the lemon juice and olive oil. Set aside to marinate for 15 minutes.

To make the cucumber salad, combine the cucumber, yoghurt and mint in a bowl and season with a little salt and pepper. Set aside.

Preheat the griller or a char-grill pan to hot. Cook the scampi, flesh-side down, for 1–2 minutes, then turn and grill the shell side for 2–3 minutes. Transfer to a platter and dress with the cucumber salad. Serve immediately.    *Serves 6*

Note: Popular in the Italian *cucina*, especially in the north, scampi are crustaceans that are closely related to prawns. They resemble small rock lobsters and have delicate, sweet flesh. New Zealand scampi are available frozen in Australia.

*The Sicilians do large fish extremely well, and this dish certainly has that southern style about it. The hotplate caramelises the flesh and gives it a lovely toasty flavour, while the stuffing seasons and moistens the fish.*

500 g swordfish fillets (*see* Note)
4 × 15 cm long sprigs rosemary
extra-virgin olive oil
1 lemon, cut into 5 mm slices
sea salt
freshly ground black pepper

*Stuffing*
2 cups dried breadcrumbs
½ cup pine nuts
½ cup sultanas
½ cup freshly grated Parmigiano-Reggiano
½ clove garlic, crushed
½ teaspoon finely chopped fresh chilli
grated zest of 1 lemon
1 teaspoon freshly chopped coriander leaves
1 tablespoon freshly chopped flat-leaf parsley
200 ml extra-virgin olive oil
sea salt
freshly ground black pepper

# Involtini di pesce spada

## SWORDFISH ROLLS WITH PINE NUTS AND SULTANAS

To make the stuffing, combine all the ingredients in a large bowl and mix well.

Cut the swordfish fillets into 3 mm thick slices, then lay the slices on a chopping board. Cover one side of each swordfish slice with an even layer of stuffing, then roll up to enclose the stuffing. Slide 3 swordfish rolls onto each rosemary sprig, then brush the rolls with a little olive oil.

Preheat the griller or a chargrill pan to hot. Put the lemon slices onto the grill plate. Add the swordfish rolls and grill for about 3 minutes on each side, rubbing with the lemon and seasoning with salt and pepper as you go. Serve immediately.   *Serves 6*

Note: These rolls work well with marlin as an alternative to swordfish.

# Contorni

*Contorni* means 'surrounding' or 'on the side', and the idea of *contorni* is to round off a meal. These are dishes that complement the mains on the dining table, giving a more structured dinner or lunch. I like to have a spread of different side dishes in the middle of the table.

Although *contorni* are side dishes, they're not necessarily any less important than other parts of the meal. Too many times they are left to the last minute and put together quickly, without much thought. But with a little creativity you can create something delicious that stands up on its own.

For this section I've picked some lovely, traditional things that are close to my heart, like *carciofi alla romana* (page 117). Oven-cooked *carciofi*, or artichokes, have been done in my family for many, many years in this Roman style. I remember that as soon as the artichoke season started, they became part of the dinner table at home. Dad was fanatical about artichokes, so we always had little ones for pickling and preserving, and big ones for cooking either as a side dish or an entrée. As a young cook in the kitchen at Dad's restaurant, I would see boxes and boxes of artichokes arrive – which meant a lot of fiddly work, peeling them vigorously so that all of the outer tough leaves were gone to leave the beautiful, soft centre. Preparing a small number of artichokes for home is less daunting.

I've also included fennel with blue cheese (*see* page 118), and some broad beans (*see* page 115). Whenever I visit southern Italy, where my father came from, I go to see my namesake, Uncle Gaetano. Apart from growing his own grapevine for making wine, he grows vegetables, including his much-loved broad beans. Out of season Uncle Gaetano and his family buy dried broad beans and reconstitute them to make a delicious broad bean purée that is eaten with olive oil and the very dense bread common to that region. Fresh broad beans are lovely, too, when double-shelled out of their pods and their second skin, and quickly pan-tossed.

*Broad beans can be cooked in a very rustic manner or dressed up to be quite elegant. This is a really tasty way of doing them, and the big flavours here make them a perfect accompaniment to a robust meal in the style of southern Italy, such as a favourite of mine, roast suckling pig (see page 149).*

500 g fresh broad beans, shelled
2½ tablespoons olive oil
1 onion, diced
1 clove garlic, finely chopped
2 tablespoons tomato paste
1 teaspoon freshly crushed basil
1 tablespoon freshly chopped flat-leaf parsley
100 ml white wine
400 ml Chicken Stock (see page 20)
salt
freshly ground black pepper (optional)

# Fave brasate

## BRAISED BROAD BEANS

Bring a large pot of salted water to the boil. Add the broad beans. When the water returns to the boil, remove the beans and refresh quickly in cold water. Slip each bean out of its tough second skin.

Wipe out the pot, then add the olive oil. Sauté the onion and garlic over a medium heat until lightly coloured. Add the broad beans, tomato paste, herbs, white wine and stock and bring to the boil. Reduce the heat and simmer for 20–30 minutes or until the broad beans are tender. Add salt and pepper, if desired. Serve immediately.    *Serves 6*

*The artichoke is a member of the thistle family, and there are many varieties, some of which have thorns and some of which do not. The Romans, whose local variety is the thornless Romanesco, have adored artichokes for centuries, and this dish, with its lemon, mint and olive oil, typifies their* cucina. *I had artichokes cooked in this fashion in a trattoria in Rome's Campo dei Fiori where they didn't even warm them up – just gave them to me as they were, from the tray that had come from the oven a couple of hours earlier. Wow! The artichoke is very closely related to the cardoon* (cardo), *and cardoons can be substituted for artichokes in this recipe with delicious results.*

# Carciofi alla romana

### ROMAN-STYLE ARTICHOKES

1 lemon
water
12 artichokes (see Note)
½ cup freshly chopped flat-leaf parsley
2 tablespoons freshly chopped sage
2 tablespoons freshly chopped mint
1 clove garlic, finely chopped
1 cup freshly grated Parmigiano-Reggiano
3 cups dried breadcrumbs
½ teaspoon freshly chopped chilli
extra-virgin olive oil
sea salt
freshly ground black pepper
1 cup white wine

 Preheat the oven to 180°C. Grate the zest from the lemon and set the zest aside. Cut the lemon in half and squeeze the juice into a large bowl of cold water. Take an artichoke and cut off the 'beard' at the base. Peel off the outside layer of leaves, then cut a small slice from the top so that the centre leaves are visible. Put the trimmed artichoke into the bowl of water to prevent discoloration. Repeat with the remaining artichokes.

In a bowl, combine the herbs, garlic, Parmigiano-Reggiano, breadcrumbs, reserved lemon zest, chilli and 300 ml olive oil. Season with salt and pepper and mix well.

Drain the artichokes, then stuff each one generously with the breadcrumb mixture by separating the leaves a little and pushing in the stuffing. Arrange the stuffed artichokes in a baking tray so that they are tightly packed in. Drizzle with olive oil, then pour in the white wine and enough water to just cover the artichokes. Season with salt and pepper. Cover with aluminium foil and bake for about 20 minutes or until the artichoke centres are tender when pierced with a skewer.   *Serves 6–12*

Note: Either the large purple spiky-leafed artichokes or the green ones are sublime cooked this way, and they make a fantastic first course as well as a side dish.

*You will love the pungent aroma and full flavour of this dish. The fresh, clean flavour of the fennel holds up very well against the strong flavour of the cheese.*

## Finocchio al gorgonzola

BAKED FENNEL WITH GORGONZOLA

4 bulbs fennel, quartered
100 ml cream
200 ml Chicken Stock
 (*see* page 20) *or*
 Vegetable Stock (*see* page 20)
250 g gorgonzola dolce latte, broken into pieces
sea salt
freshly ground black pepper

Preheat the oven to 180° C. Arrange the fennel in a baking tray and cover with the cream and stock. Put a piece of gorgonzola on each piece of fennel, then season with salt and pepper. Bake for 15 minutes or until the fennel is tender and slightly browned on top.   *Serves 6*

*Braised cabbage is great with pork and other rich meats, but it is so tasty you could have it on its own. Try it with different types of cabbage until you discover everybody's favourite.*

## Cavolo stufato

BRAISED CABBAGE

50 ml olive oil
2 onions, finely diced
3 cloves garlic, chopped
1 carrot, finely diced
2 celery stalks, finely diced
200 g bacon, diced
1 cabbage, shredded
2 tablespoons freshly chopped sage
2 cups Chicken Stock
 (*see* page 20) *or*
 Vegetable Stock (*see* page 20)

Heat the olive oil in a large, heavy-based pot. Cook the onion and garlic over a moderate heat for 3–4 minutes until the onion is soft, then add the carrot, celery and bacon and cook for 2 minutes. Add the cabbage and sage and mix well. Cover and cook for 5 minutes, stirring occasionally. Pour in the stock and cook, covered, for 20–25 minutes until the cabbage is soft and most of the liquid has evaporated.   *Serves 10*

*Opposite:* Finocchio al Gorgonzola

*This is one of the simplest and tastiest ways of doing spuds. They're great at any meal. Best of all are the little golden bits that form on the hot surface of the pan during cooking and have to be scraped off. Try different potato varieties here – I like rich, waxy potatoes that have some weight, like Spuntas.*

# Patate fritte

## ITALIAN FRIED POTATOES

Put the potatoes into a large pot and cover with water. Add a little salt and bring to the boil. Cook for about 20 minutes or until the potatoes are soft but not falling apart. Drain and allow to cool.

Peel the potatoes and chop into large cubes. Heat a generous amount of olive oil (but not as much as you would use if deep-frying) in a large, deep pan. Add the potato, garlic and rosemary and sauté until golden, seasoning with salt and pepper while cooking. Serve immediately.   *Serves 6*

8 large waxy potatoes, unpeeled
sea salt
olive oil
8 cloves garlic, unpeeled
leaves from 4 sprigs rosemary
freshly ground black pepper

The word says it all – *improvviso*, meaning 'sudden'. How many times have you felt caught out by unexpected arrivals, when your culinary prowess has suddenly been put to the test? Or perhaps you've had to make a late decision on a meal, or even simply had a spot of the munchies. Whatever the case, a well-stocked pantry will save you. Inspiration can be gathered by simply opening the cupboard door – just like when you go to the market and get inspired by what's available.

A versatile pantry means you don't have to have a planned menu to create wonderful dishes. And when you combine items in your pantry with fresh ingredients you add another dimension to your cooking. Fill your pantry with products that become precious to you – your favourite oil, your favourite pastas – and you'll always be prepared.

The pantry is a very important part of the Italian *cucina*, because a lot of the staples are kept there – your beautiful olive oils, your dry pastas, rice, beans and preserves. If you keep your cupboard well stocked, you'll have an unplanned banquet before you. You can take some lovely anchovies, some olive oil and a bag of a pasta, and throw together a *spaghetti aglio e olio*. I guess it's the Italian version of fast food – quick and easy, but very good for you; wholesome and real.

In this chapter there are recipes for quick and tasty pasta dishes as well as interesting risotti and simple bruschetta. I've also included some preserves, such as *carciofi* and *melanzane*, which have been favourites in my family for years. It adds a bit of depth to your pantry to have a few things you've

prepared in advance when you've had the inclination or the time. They're ready to go, which is especially good when you're in a hurry. You can of course *buy* preserves and the like, but it feels great to make your own.

What does a well-stocked pantry contain? It can be anything, but there are a few must-haves – the sorts of things any self-respecting Italian boy or girl would never be caught without. Here are a few notes to get you started. Think of them as a shopping list.

**Dry pasta**: There are companies that produce commercial dry pasta in bulk, and then there are smaller, more artisan-style *pastifici*, which produce and pack their pasta by hand and generally use higher-quality ingredients. Obviously, the higher-quality product commands a higher price – we're talking about $6 or $7 a kilo compared with $2 for lesser-quality pasta. I believe it's worth it. At least explore both options and see if you feel the price difference is justified. If you're happy with the cheaper one, then go for it. Southern Italians embrace pasta more completely than the rest of the country (in fact, Sicilians use the word *maccheroni* to describe any mixture of flour and water, and maybe eggs), and many Italian pasta factories are in the south. While fresh pasta is perhaps made at home or in a restaurant, generally when Italians are consuming pasta, they're eating the dry version.

**Olive oil**: Olive oil is the beginning of nearly all of the fundamental recipes of the Italian *cucina*. It imparts as much flavour to frying onions as it does when poured directly onto a salad as a dressing. Oil that is simply labelled 'olive oil' will usually be a blend of virgin olive oil and refined oil, and, while it may not have strong nutty or grassy flavours like virgin or extra-virgin olive oil, it's fine for frying and a must for the pantry. Extra-virgin olive oil, unprocessed oil of a top grade, is known as the best. To be classified as 'extra-virgin', it must have an acid level of below 1 gram per 100 g, or 1 per cent. 'Virgin' olive oil must have an acid level of not more than 2 per cent, but must still have a perfect aroma, flavour and colour. Unlike with wine, the labels on olive oil bottles feature little or no description to guide you. As a general rule of thumb, the further south in Italy you go, the stronger and more pungent the oil becomes. Australia is now producing some excellent extra-virgin olive oils with their own unique flavours, but ultimately your own tastebuds should be your guide. It's great to keep a number of different oils on hand, but remember that olive oil should be stored away from the light.

**Polenta**: Polenta is a staple in the diets of northern Italians, so my mother, who is from that part of the country, makes it often. Cornmeal or dried maize is ground to a coarse, medium or fine consistency, then poured into boiling salted water and stirred constantly until it thickens. I prefer a finer-grain polenta as I like the smoother texture in my mouth. It's the perfect accompaniment for a rich *spezzatino* (stew) or a hearty wet roast. Polenta is not always golden yellow – it also comes in a white variety, and there is a buckwheat polenta called *taragna* that is prepared in the same way as traditional polenta but provides an interesting alternative taste.

**Rice**: In Italy, rice is to the north as pasta is to the south. Always use an arborio rice to make risotto – no other variety will perform as well. *Super fino* and *fino* are the best of the arborio rices. The grains are short and round, and absorb up to two and a half times their mass in liquid. It's best to use rice that has been milled by hand if possible, as it will have the smallest number of broken grains. This is important because it affects the absorption of liquid during the cooking process. When buying rice, where possible pour some into the palm of your hand and check for the number of broken grains to get an idea of the quality of the producer and how the rice has been milled.

**Preserves**: *Sotto olio* (preserved in oil), *sotto aceto* (vinegar) and *sotto liquore* (alcohol) are always well represented in the Italian larder. These preserves are age-old methods of storing food, created by necessity due to surplus production. Being able to enjoy fruit out of season makes the effort of bottling them worthwhile, not to mention how good they look lined up, with their wonderful colours. Such a display is an obvious sign of the ability of a cook. Fruit and vegetables in jars can always be found on my shelves, ranging from peaches in liqueur to eggplants and wild mushrooms in vinegar and oil.

**Canned tomatoes**: I always buy canned Italian tomatoes in bulk, even for home. I find them richer in flavour and redder in colour than other tomatoes, and I'm always in search of the tastiest tomato I can find. I buy them chopped or whole, rather than crushed, so that when they are cooked you can still see the tomato.

**Tuna**: It is surprising just how versatile canned tuna can be. The quality available varies widely. Try to buy the best quality you can afford – and it must preferably be in olive oil, which is moister than tuna in brine. However, if the tuna is of a high quality, it can be very good in brine, too.

**Anchovies**: Good-quality anchovies are one of the tastiest little morsels that can be found. The better-quality the anchovy, the less salt used in the preserving process, which allows you to taste the fish rather than the processing method.

**Capers**: I like to keep capers in my pantry, especially the smaller ones, as they can be added to many dishes to boost the flavour.

**Olives**: There is a world of olives available now, in all shapes and sizes. Some are marinated and others are filled with anything from goat's cheese to sun-dried tomato. Whether your chosen olives are stored in a glass jar or a vacuum-sealed bag, they can be made into a delightful nibble by adding a few ingredients of your own. Try a combination of herbs, garlic, lemon juice and spices to create a taste of your own.

**Dried mushrooms**: I always have bags of dried mushrooms on hand. Porcini and chanterelles (*galletti*) have an intense, yeasty flavour I really enjoy adding to my cooking. The flavours really liven up a braised dish. Remember when soaking mushrooms to beware of stones and grit, which can gather at the bottom of the bowl – but don't discard the liquid, as it contains a great deal of flavour.

*Bruschetta is easy yet rewarding. You can feed plenty of people quickly, and they will love it. Whatever you do, the key is to use good basic ingredients. One simple food becomes the highlight, like the anchovies here. I like to use the wonderful Ortiz brand of anchovies.*

## Bruschetta con acciughe e capperi

### BRUSCHETTA WITH ANCHOVIES AND CAPERS

1 loaf rustic-style bread
1 clove garlic, peeled
4 anchovy fillets, cut in half lengthwise
1 tablespoon capers
½ cup freshly chopped flat-leaf parsley
sea salt
freshly ground black pepper
100 ml extra-virgin olive oil

Cut the bread into 5 mm thick slices (allow 2 slices per person). Grill or toast the bread on both sides, then rub 1 side with the garlic. Top with anchovy, spoon on some capers and sprinkle with parsley. Season with salt and pepper, drizzle with olive oil and serve.   *Serves 4*

*Preserved eggplant is great to have on hand for antipasto. When following this recipe it is important to allow the eggplant slices to sit overnight – any excess moisture and bitterness will be reduced greatly.*

## Melanzane sotto olio

### PRESERVED EGGPLANT IN OIL

2 kg eggplants, peeled
salt
4 whole cloves garlic
5 mint leaves
300 ml good-quality white vinegar
600 ml extra-virgin olive oil

Cut the eggplants into 5 cm × 6 cm × 5 mm slices. Sprinkle with a little salt, then put into a colander set over a bowl. Cover with a lid and put a weight on top. Leave overnight in a cool place.

Next day, put the eggplant into sterilised jars (there is no need to rinse off the salt). Tuck some garlic and mint into each jar, then cover with 1 part vinegar to 2 parts oil. Put the lids on tightly. Store for at least 1 week before use. The preserved eggplant will keep for at least 1 year.

*Opposite: Bruschetta con Acciughe e Capperi*

*When the season comes, I love to preserve baby artichokes, so that I can draw on them when they are not around fresh. It's a bit time-consuming, but wonderfully satisfying to have them whenever I want to use them.*

# Carciofi sotto olio

## PRESERVED ARTICHOKES IN OIL

Cut the zest from the lemon, then cut it into strips and set aside. Cut the lemon in half and squeeze the juice into a large bowl of cold water. Take an artichoke and cut off the stem close to the base. Remove the tough outside leaves, then cut a small slice from the top so that the centre leaves are visible. Put the trimmed artichoke into the bowl of water to prevent discoloration. Repeat with the remaining artichokes.

In a large pot, combine the vinegar with an equal quantity of water to make a brine. Season well with salt, then bring to the boil. Drain the artichokes and transfer to the pot. Boil for 10 minutes, then remove the artichokes from the brine and put into a large bowl. Add the reserved lemon zest and the chilli, season with pepper and mix well. Put into sterilised jars and cover with olive oil. Seal the jars tightly with proper lids. Return them to the wiped-out pot and pour in enough clean water to come up to the lids. Boil the jars for 20 minutes, then allow to cool – this process will form an airtight seal. Store the preserved artichokes in a cool place. They will keep for at least 1 year.

Note: With a bit of notice, your greengrocer should be able to organise baby artichokes with their grower.

zest from 2 lemons, cut into strips
2 kg baby artichokes (*see* Note)
2 litres white-wine vinegar
sea salt
1 fresh chilli, seeded and finely chopped
freshly ground black pepper
1 litre olive oil
water

*Chris and I made up this dish years ago. We had preserved artichokes, and it just seemed natural to add the olive paste and the spaghetti. 'Tasted very Italian,' actor Steve Martin wrote on our menu.*

500 g spaghettini
   (preferably Martelli)
salt
300 g black olives (*see* Note)
olive oil
350 g Preserved Artichokes
   (*see* page 128)
1 clove garlic, chopped
freshly cracked black pepper
1 teaspoon freshly chopped
   chilli
pinch of dried oregano
freshly grated Parmigiano-
   Reggiano
freshly chopped
   flat-leaf parsley

# Spaghettini con carciofi e olive

## SPAGHETTINI WITH ARTICHOKES AND OLIVE PASTE

Cook the spaghettini in plenty of salted boiling water until al dente. Meanwhile, pip the olives and purée the flesh in a blender with a dash of olive oil. Cut the preserved artichokes into quarters or bite-sized pieces.

Heat some olive oil in a pan and lightly sauté the garlic. Add the artichoke pieces and season with a little salt and pepper (the olives will only intensify the saltiness, so you can adjust the seasoning again later if necessary). Stir in the chilli and oregano, then toss through the cooked spaghettini. Add the Parmigiano-Reggiano and the puréed olives and, using a fork, mix evenly through the pasta. Sprinkle with parsley and serve.   *Serves 4*

Note: Greek kalamata olives, which have a stronger flavour than Italian olives, are good here. If you prefer a more subtle flavour, use Ligurian olives.

*For an unusual and spectacular serving dish for this pasta, use a hollowed-out Parmigiano-Reggiano rind, as in the photograph opposite.*

# Spaghetti alla carrettiera

SPAGHETTI WITH TUNA AND PORCINI MUSHROOMS

100 g dried porcini,
    soaked overnight
2½ tablespoons olive oil
½ onion, finely chopped
2 cloves garlic, finely chopped
60 g pancetta slices, chopped
1 stick celery, finely sliced
2 tablespoons tomato paste
sea salt
freshly ground black pepper
1 × 500 g can crushed tomatoes
1 teaspoon freshly crushed basil
1 tablespoon freshly chopped
    flat-leaf parsley
1 × 80 g can tuna in oil
500 g spaghetti

Lift the porcini from their soaking liquid and drain. Heat the olive oil in a heavy-based pot. Add the onion, garlic, pancetta and celery and sauté over a medium heat for 4–5 minutes, stirring continuously. Add the tomato paste and porcini and cook for 3–4 minutes, stirring to avoid sticking. Season with salt and pepper, then add the tomatoes, basil and parsley and cook for 20–30 minutes, uncovered, over a medium–low heat, stirring occasionally. Drain the tuna, then add to the pot and cook gently for 5 minutes.

    Cook the spaghetti in plenty of well-salted boiling water until al dente. Drain. Toss the pasta with the sauce and serve immediately.  *Serves 4*

*Perfect for an* improvviso *situation, this sauce gets cooked often at my house. I enjoy it with potato gnocchi, but penne is also frequently requested.*

# Penne matriciana

2½ tablespoons olive oil
1 onion, finely chopped
1 stick celery, finely chopped
1 clove garlic, finely chopped
2 teaspoons Basil Pesto (*see* page 18)
1 teaspoon freshly chopped oregano
1–2 teaspoons freshly chopped chilli
250 g pork cheek (*see* page 67)
    *or* pancetta, thinly sliced
2½ tablespoons tomato paste
100 ml white wine
1 × 500 g can good-quality
    whole peeled tomatoes
2 bay leaves
sea salt
freshly ground black pepper
500 g penne *or* other dry pasta
freshly grated Parmigiano-Reggiano

Heat the oil in a large pot, then add the onion, celery, garlic, pesto, oregano and chilli and sauté gently. Add the pork cheek and sauté for a few minutes. Add the tomato paste and cook for a few minutes, then deglaze the pot with the wine. Pass the tomatoes through a food mill or fine sieve and add to the pot, mixing well. Add the bay leaves and season with a little salt and pepper. Simmer for 15 minutes.

    Cook the penne in plenty of well-salted boiling water until al dente, then drain. Combine with the sauce and serve immediately with Parmigiano-Reggiano.  *Serves 4*

*Opposite:* Spaghetti alla Carrettiera

*Risotto originates in northern Italy, and opinions vary on how best to make it. My 'family' method of making it is the same as that used by my friend Gabriele Ferron from the Riseria Ferron company in Italy.*

1 tablespoon olive oil
1 onion, finely chopped
1 clove garlic, finely chopped
50 g dried porcini mushrooms,
    soaked overnight (*see* Note)
3 cups arborio rice
pinch of freshly chopped sage
sea salt
freshly ground black pepper
1.25 litres Chicken Stock
    (*see* page 20)
50 g butter
1 cup freshly grated Parmigiano-
    Reggiano

# Risotto con porcini

## RISOTTO WITH PORCINI MUSHROOMS

Heat the oil in a heavy-based saucepan and gently sauté the onion and garlic until soft. Lift the porcini from their soaking liquid and drain. Add to the saucepan over a high heat and stir to combine. Add the rice and sage, then season with salt and pepper and cook for 3–5 minutes. Stir in the stock. Bring to the boil, then lower the heat and simmer for 20 minutes, stirring occasionally, until the rice has soaked up most of the liquid and is tender but not too soft. Add the butter and cheese and stir until creamy. Serve immediately. *Serves 4*

Note: Be sure to lift the mushrooms out of the soaking liquid to ensure that the dirt stays at the bottom and does not end up in the risotto. For extra flavour and boost, strain the mushroom-soaking liquid and substitute it for some of the stock.

*Midnight-snack magic: simple, quick and light. Use your best olive oil.*

500 g spaghetti
salt
100 ml extra-virgin olive oil
2 cloves garlic, finely chopped
pinch of freshly chopped chilli
1 teaspoon capers
freshly ground black pepper
½ cup freshly chopped
    flat-leaf parsley

# Spaghetti aglio e olio

## SPAGHETTI WITH GARLIC AND OLIVE OIL

Cook the spaghetti in plenty of well-salted boiling water until al dente. Meanwhile, heat the oil in a large frying pan and add the garlic, chilli and capers. Season to taste with salt and pepper. Cook over a medium heat for a few minutes but do not let the garlic colour too much. Drain the pasta, then add it to the frying pan. Add the parsley and toss well. Serve immediately. *Serves 4*

*Opposite page: Risotto con Porcini*

*A traditional dish that is not very well known, this Tuscan risotto surprises with its unusual use of strawberries as a savoury flavour. If you can obtain little wild strawberries, it is even better.*

# Risotto con le fragole

## SAVOURY STRAWBERRY RISOTTO

⅓ cup olive oil
1 leek (white part only),
   finely chopped and well washed
200 g small strawberries
sea salt
freshly ground black pepper
3 cups arborio rice
¼ cup white wine
1.25 litres Chicken Stock
   (see page 20)
100 g freshly grated Asiago cheese
   (see Note)
50 g butter

Heat the olive oil in a large, heavy-based pot. Add the leek and sauté over a medium heat until soft and sweet smelling. Add half the strawberries and season with salt and pepper. Cook until soft, stirring occasionally. Add the rice and mix well until it takes on a brighter white colour. Stir in the white wine, then the stock. Reduce the heat and simmer for 20 minutes or until the rice is cooked. Add a little more stock, if necessary.

Add the cheese and butter and the remaining strawberries, stirring until creamy. Taste and, if necessary, add salt and pepper (a little more black pepper will give the risotto a sharper flavour). Serve immediately.   *Serves 4*

Note: Asiago is a firm cow's-milk cheese that takes its name from a town in the Veneto region of Italy. It has a subtle, sweet flavour and melts well when heated. The cheese is available in Australia at good delicatessens and cheese shops.

# Loaves and Fishes

My father was born in Puglia, in southern Italy, and Mum was born in Verona, in the north – so they were an eclectic mix. They met in Milan and came to Australia in 1960 to start a family. At first, we grew up in Melbourne as a basic nuclear family – we had no cousins, aunts, uncles, grandparents, nothing. But with every birth there had to be a godfather or godmother – a *compare* or *comare* – and it wasn't long before they become our extended family.

In the Italian family calendar there are always days that are cause for celebration, and there are usually a lot of people to help celebrate. Your family may be small, but as the years go on, it grows and grows (and grows). With every family we joined came more children, more births, more marriages, more communions, and bigger Easter and Christmas celebrations. It's very rare to have a get-together at my house with fewer than twenty people – and that's just the immediate family and pretty close friends. Friends are family, and family are friends.

The 'Main Event' chapter was about the meal as special occasion, but 'Loaves and Fishes' is the truly full-blown celebration. The story of Venice typifies this attitude. Many, many years ago, Venice was a famous trading destination for the Middle East and a thriving metropolis, but eventually the trade stopped and the city suffered an economic downturn. So the doges, the city's leaders, invented a carnival to lift the people's spirits. It worked well, so they had another, and Venice eventually became the city of carnivals. Today, if you look at the Venetian calendar, there are more days of the year when they're

# Al Fresco

having a carnival than not. The city has survived for a thousand years on its huge tourist trade because of the people's attitude that they were going to have fun regardless of the state of the economy.

A lot of that attitude comes through in aspects of the Italian celebration, when big families come together. In this chapter I deal with preparing food for large numbers of people, including a couple of dishes typically made for particular special occasions.

When cooking for large groups, you need to keep in mind what will work in your environment, with your tools. It can be difficult if you haven't got a large stove or oven, but a barbecue can be a great solution. Otherwise, you can always turn to the 'Cool Food' chapter – one of the greatest things you can do for a crowd is provide a huge spread of *antipasti*, and it also frees you to prepare other dishes without having to serve up the first course. You'll also find some great ideas for feeding large groups in other chapters, such as 'The Prince and the Pauper'.

I've included some 'outdoor' dishes in the following pages, because with large numbers it's very appealing to entertain *al fresco*, where there's more space. We've got beautiful weather here in Melbourne during the summertime and spring, and it's great to get people outdoors. I think Melburnians really love doing this, and the Italian culture embraces that kind of eating as well, especially when it's a big *festa*. It's lovely being outside with the smell of things roasting and beautiful salads set up.

*Eggs appear in so many dishes that it is often forgotten how good they can be as a main ingredient. With a little thought they can be built into a range of beautiful, simple dishes, including frittata. There are many different flavourings that can be used in frittata: the humble potato is one of my favourites.*

# Frittata di patate

## POTATO FRITTATA

2 large potatoes, diced
olive oil
sea salt
freshly ground black pepper
1 medium onion, chopped
6 eggs
50 ml cream
1 cup freshly grated Parmigiano-Reggiano
1 tablespoon freshly chopped flat-leaf parsley
1 teaspoon freshly chopped sage

Preheat the oven to 180°C. Put the potato into a roasting tray and sprinkle with olive oil. Season with salt and pepper and bake for about 15 minutes, mixing from time to time, until golden brown. Remove from the oven (leave the oven on) and allow to cool.

Heat a little olive oil in a frying pan and sauté the onion over a medium heat until soft and golden. Remove from the heat and allow to cool.

Put the eggs and cream into a bowl and beat until well combined. Add the Parmigiano-Reggiano and herbs and season with salt and pepper. Mix through the cooled potato and onion. Heat 1 tablespoon olive oil in a deep ovenproof frying pan, then add the egg mixture and stir for 1–2 minutes or until the frittata begins to set. Put the pan into the oven for about 10 minutes until the frittata is golden brown and just firm to touch in the centre.

Cut into slices and serve immediately, or allow to cool and serve at room temperature or cold.   *Serves 4*

12 large green prawns,
   shelled and de-veined
flour
50 ml olive oil
200 g green beans,
   blanched
200 g cherry tomatoes
1 clove garlic, chopped
1 tablespoon freshly chopped
   flat-leaf parsley
1 fresh red chilli,
   seeded and chopped
juice of 1 lime
100 ml olive oil
sea salt
freshly ground black pepper

*Although I have used prawns here, this dish is great with all crustaceans. I like to let it cool without refrigerating it – the flavour is far more intense this way.*

# Insalata di gamberi

## FRIED PRAWN SALAD

Dust the prawns lightly in flour and shake off the excess. Heat the oil in a frying pan or wok and fry the prawns over a high heat for about 2 minutes until golden brown. Lift the prawns from the oil and put them into a bowl. Add the remaining ingredients and mix well. Transfer to a large platter and allow to cool. Serve at room temperature.   *Serves 6*

500 g homemade orecchiette
   (*see* page 67)
salt
olive oil
3 large tomatoes,
   halved, seeded and diced
handful of basil leaves, shredded
1 clove garlic, finely sliced
1 teaspoon freshly chopped chilli
½ cup freshly chopped
   flat-leaf parsley
1 teaspoon dried oregano
   (optional)
100 ml extra-virgin olive oil
freshly ground black pepper

*You do not have to use* orecchiette *for this dish (penne is also good), but its fantastic rustic texture is well worth the effort. What a summer's treat, with the tomato and basil and the flavour of excellent olive oil!*

# Pasta di casa in insalata

## SALAD OF HOMEMADE PASTA WITH TOMATO AND BASIL

Cook the *orecchiette* in plenty of salted boiling water for about 7 minutes or until al dente. Drain and put on a tray to cool. Drizzle with a little oil while still warm, stir through lightly and set aside.

Combine the *orecchiette*, tomatoes and basil in a large bowl. Add the remaining ingredients and toss well. Season with salt and pepper and serve.   *Serves 4*

*Opposite page:* Insalata di Gamberi

*Crumbed veal is one of the easiest things in the world, and everybody loves it. It tastes great hot or cold, so is ideal for a picnic. Serve it with an accompaniment of your choice – I love mashed potato and a simple tomato-and-onion salad (see page 54).*

# Cotoletta alla milanese

### PAN-FRIED CRUMBED VEAL

Lay a veal slice on your workbench and cover with a sheet of plastic wrap. Beat gently with a meat mallet until the slice is no thicker than 5 mm. Dust with flour on both sides and shake off the excess. Season the egg with salt and pepper. Dip the veal into the egg, then the breadcrumbs, pressing the crumbs down firmly to ensure an even crust. Set aside on a tray. Repeat with each piece of veal. (When layering the pieces of crumbed veal on the tray, put extra breadcrumbs between the layers so that the pieces do not stick to each other.)

Heat the olive oil in a large frying pan. Cook the veal in batches so that each piece has enough space to fry evenly. Fry one side over a medium heat for 2–3 minutes until golden, then turn over and cook the other side. Drain on kitchen paper, then season with a little salt and serve hot, warm or cold with wedges of lemon and your chosen accompaniment. Yum!
*Serves 6*

1 kg veal loin *or* topside, thinly sliced
flour
4 eggs, beaten
sea salt
freshly ground black pepper
4 cups dried breadcrumbs
300 ml olive oil
lemon wedges

*This salad is of Neapolitan origin. Family friends first put me on to it, and it has been a favourite ever since. You will love the sharp, minty flavour of the dressed zucchini with the mozzarella.*

# Insalata di zucchini con mozzarella di bufalo

## SALAD OF ZUCCHINI AND BUFFALO-MILK MOZZARELLA

2 eggs

½ cup freshly grated Parmigiano-Reggiano

1 tablespoon freshly chopped flat-leaf parsley

400 ml olive oil

2 medium zucchini, cut into 3 mm thick slices

flour

1 tablespoon freshly chopped mint

1 clove garlic, chopped

sea salt

freshly ground black pepper

300 g buffalo-milk mozzarella, finely sliced

 Break the eggs into a bowl, then add the Parmigiano-Reggiano and parsley and beat well. Heat three quarters of the oil in a large frying pan until hot. Dust the zucchini slices in flour, shake off the excess and dip into the egg mixture. Fry the zucchini in batches over a high heat for about a minute on each side until golden brown. Drain on kitchen paper. Transfer the zucchini to a shallow dish and scatter over the mint and garlic. Drizzle with the remaining oil and season with salt and pepper. Let stand for 10 minutes.

Put a layer of zucchini into a serving dish, then cover with a layer of mozzarella slices. Repeat with the remaining zucchini and cheese, finishing with a layer of zucchini. Refrigerate for several hours before serving.   *Serves 4*

# The Feast

It can be impressive to serve fewer dishes, but in larger quantities – it provides a great sense of abundance. For example, the fried prawn salad in the 'Al Fresco' section (see page 140) could be made in a big quantity and served on a huge platter. A few centrepieces like this look great, and cut down the workload a bit, too. That's why I love things like the beautiful suckling pig on page 149, which is an Italian Christmas classic. You've got this beast that's been cooked in an almost sacrificial way, and it looks big, appetising and succulent.

It's the same with the big roasted fish on page 146. This is a fantastic Good Friday dish when you can't have meat. Church is always late on Good Friday – it starts at about 3 p.m. and finishes about 4 p.m. – and there's fasting all morning, so by four o'clock everybody's ravenous. There's a (respectful) race from the church back to home, to get into the fish.

With dishes like these, I think people love to get in there and pull bits off, which makes for a very enjoyable occasion. People have to interact – they're helping themselves and helping others, getting a plate for Dad or whoever. If a dish is a bit fiddly it just won't work in this sort of situation where you've got everyone having a go at it. It has to be quite robust, so we're looking at a simpler type of cookery.

*Eggplants are particularly sweet when cooked this way after having been salted overnight to bring out the bitterness and extra moisture. I like to use large black eggplants so that I can cut through the layers neatly once they have been cooked in the oven.*

# Melanzane alla parmigiana

## EGGPLANT PARMIGIANA

4 large eggplants
salt
200 ml olive oil
1 litre Tomato Sauce (see page 18)
3 large buffalo-milk mozzarella, thinly sliced
10 freshly chopped basil leaves
1 teaspoon freshly chopped oregano
1 cup freshly grated Parmigiano-Reggiano
freshly ground black pepper

Cut the eggplants crossways into slices. Sprinkle with a little salt, then put into a colander set over a bowl. Cover with a lid and put a weight on top. Leave overnight in a cool place.

Next day, preheat the oven to 180°C. Rinse the salt off the eggplant slices and pat dry. Heat a little of the olive oil in a large frying pan and gently fry the eggplant in batches on both sides until slightly golden, adding more oil as needed. Drain on kitchen paper.

Arrange a layer of eggplant in an ovenproof dish (this can be the serving dish), then cover sparingly with tomato sauce. Cover with mozzarella slices and scatter with some of the herbs and Parmigiano-Reggiano. Repeat with the remaining eggplant, tomato sauce and mozzarella, finishing with a layer of mozzarella and Parmigiano-Reggiano. Season with pepper. Bake until the top is golden. Take the dish directly to the table to serve, or serve individual portions in the usual way.   *Serves 10*

*What a great way to do fish. Roasting it whole ensures the maximum moisture is retained, and with the addition of some tasty herb-and-spice paste, the flavour is enhanced. The aromatics and oil in the paste permeate the flesh of the fish, and the smells and visual impact when you present the dish at the feasting table are fantastic. Make sure your oven can accommodate the fish you buy – I have been caught out in the past! In such cases I have used the barbecue and it has worked well.*

1 onion, sliced
1 stick celery, sliced
1 × 3 kg snapper (see Note), cleaned and scaled
2 lemons
200 ml verjuice
2½ tablespoons olive oil
sea salt
freshly ground black pepper

*Paste*
2 cloves garlic, crushed
1 teaspoon freshly chopped ginger
1 teaspoon freshly chopped chilli
1 tablespoon coriander leaves
1 tablespoon freshly chopped flat-leaf parsley
1 tablespoon freshly chopped dill leaves
½ cup dried breadcrumbs (see Note)
100 ml olive oil
sea salt
freshly ground black pepper

# Pesce arrosto

## ROASTED WHOLE BIG FISH

Preheat the oven to 200°C. Scatter the onion and celery in a large baking dish and lay the fish on top. Using a sharp knife, make 3–4 incisions into the flesh of the fish on one side, about 1 cm deep. Turn the fish over and make 3–4 more incisions.

To make the paste, combine all the ingredients using a large mortar and pestle.

Rub the paste into the fish, making sure it penetrates the incisions. Slice 1 of the lemons and arrange around the fish. Cut the other lemon in half and squeeze over the juice. Drizzle the verjuice and oil over the fish, then season with salt and pepper. Bake for 30 minutes, basting every so often with the juices from the bottom of the dish. Touch with your finger to check whether the fish is cooked through – it should be firm but not springy. Take the baking dish directly to the table and allow your guests to serve themselves.   *Serves 10*

Note: I have suggested snapper here, but any of the larger, fleshy fish can be done this way. Try coral trout, barramundi or blue eye cod, just to name a few. Substitute brioche crumbs for the breadcrumbs in the paste for a richer result.

*Suckling pig is one of those special treats. For me it represents true occasion. It is rich, moist, fatty and dangerously delicious. Roasting it in this way brings out the very best of the meat, with its crackling and gamey juniper-and-anise flavour. The lemon myrtle is a great addition – very Sardinian. I first tasted pig cooked with lemon myrtle at a Sardinian restaurant in Rome, and have to say that the flavours go together beautifully. I grow my own lemon myrtle at home. The Tuscans have their own version of this dish, which they call* porchetta. *It is usually cooked on a spit* (girarrosto).

½ suckling pig
(about 4 kg; see Note)
1 onion, roughly chopped
1 carrot, roughly chopped
1 stick celery, roughly chopped
1 tablespoon freshly chopped
rosemary
1 tablespoon freshly chopped
sage
2 star anise, crushed
1 tablespoon juniper berries,
crushed
½ cup freshly chopped
lemon myrtle leaves
2 cloves garlic, crushed
200 ml olive oil
sea salt
freshly ground black pepper
400 ml Chicken Stock
(see page 20) *or*
Veal Stock (see page 19)

# Porcellino al forno

## ROAST SUCKLING PIG

Preheat the oven to 200°C. Using a boning knife, separate the front and back legs from the ribs. Using a cleaver, trim the points of the ribs. You should now have 3 pieces: the front leg, the back leg, and the rib section. (If you prefer, ask your butcher to portion the meat for you.) Scatter the onion, carrot and celery in a large baking dish. Put the pieces of pork on top of the vegetables, skin side down.

Using a mortar and pestle, combine the herbs, spices, myrtle leaves and garlic with a little of the oil to form a paste. Massage the paste into the meat, then season with salt and pepper. Turn the pork over so that the skin is facing upwards. Drizzle with the remaining oil and sprinkle with plenty of salt. Pour the stock into the bottom of the baking dish. Bake for 35–40 minutes or until the skin is hard and golden brown and the meat is cooked through. Test the meat for doneness by inserting a skewer into the thickest part. If the juices run clear, it is ready. Take the baking dish to the table for carving and serving.   *Serves 10*

Note: You will need to pre-order the suckling pig from your butcher. A large cut of pork could be substituted.

*Chestnuts are the quintessential winter's delight. Their season is very short, which makes them even more special. It is fantastic to walk down a busy city street and pass a chestnut vendor roasting the nuts over hot coals.*

# Castagne arrosto

### ROASTED CHESTNUTS

Using a sharp knife and a fair amount of pressure, score the outer skin of each chestnut with a cross. Put the scored nuts into a pan that has holes in the base and set it over an open fire. Cook for 10–15 minutes, tossing the pan to rotate the nuts and cook them evenly. Once the skin starts to peel back and the nut inside has turned a honey-golden colour, they are ready to peel and eat. (If you don't have an open fire, put the scored chestnuts on a baking tray and put them into a preheated oven at 180°C. Roast for 15–20 minutes, tossing every 5 minutes.)

Note: The pan you need for cooking the chestnuts is available at specialist cookware stores.

*Roasting sweet red peppers intensifies their flavour and enriches their appearance. Stuffing them with cheese or other ingredients, as here, makes them a more substantial offering.*

# Peperoni ripieni di fetta

### ROASTED RED PEPPERS STUFFED WITH FETTA

4 large red peppers,
　halved lengthwise and seeded
100 ml olive oil
sea salt
freshly ground black pepper
1 clove garlic, sliced
350 g fetta cheese, cubed
8 basil leaves

Preheat the oven to 180°C. Put the peppers on a baking tray, cut side up. Drizzle with the olive oil and season with salt and pepper, then sprinkle over the garlic. Bake for 15 minutes. Remove from the oven and fill each with an equal amount of fetta. Return to the oven for 5 minutes, then garnish each stuffed pepper with 1 basil leaf and serve.   *Serves 8*

*Opposite: Castagne Arrosto*

# Bread

Bread is an amazing thing. It's so simple, and people have been baking it for thousand of years. It is important in the Italian culture because, although not everybody practises rigidly, it's a big part of the religion. The bread is the Eucharist, the body of Christ. And bread is always present at meals. It was there at the Last Supper, and it's involved in every celebration. You just can't have people come around without serving bread.

A few years ago, I used to say that the first thing I do when I visit Italy is to grab an espresso coffee, then go to a restaurant and order some buffalo-milk mozzarella, a piece of bread and few slices of prosciutto from San Daniele, which is next to none in the world. The coffee would be fantastic and different from what you could get here (you couldn't get buffalo-milk mozzarella at all!), and the bread was certainly different and of a higher quality.

There was a time in Melbourne – and I'm not going back that far – when you couldn't really get great bread. If you looked hard enough you could get an okay product, but not the really beautiful, old-style bread, baked the artisan way with good grains. So in the restaurant we baked our own. Eventually we just became too busy to do it and needed to get help. I looked around and met Daniel Di Chirico. Daniel does all our restaurant bread now, making it at Baker D. Chirico in St Kilda. He's a very traditional baker, using flour made from ancient grains such as spelt, and I'm happy to report that there are a lot of bakers around town now doing that lovely style of bread.

Because of Daniel, and because we're doing things like buffalo-milk mozzarella in Australia now, that simple meal is no longer so high on my list of priorities when I visit Italy. (But San Daniele still makes the best prosciutto in the world!)

What makes a good bread? It's both the way it's made and the products used in it. These days you can buy commercial yeast and flour mixes that already have all the goodies in there,

and you just add water and bake it. That's fine, and it will give you perhaps a light, fluffy white bread with a nice crust. But bread can be more pure than that – for example, the flours don't have to be so cleaned and washed. At the restaurant we love to use an unbleached flour; it's more natural and you get a darker, slightly heavier loaf. The yeast is an important factor. Daniel makes his own yeast – from fermenting apples, for example – and he adds to it all the time and keeps it growing. In Italian we call this starter dough the *biga*. It gives that almost sour flavour to the bread and makes it more dense.

Of course, it's a lot of work to make bread this way. But there's a rewarding, sexy feeling about kneading dough with your hands on a floured board, leaving it in a corner for a couple of hours and watching it grow, then pushing it back, rolling it into shapes, watching it grow again and then finally baking it – it's a romantic thing. I guess a lot of people wouldn't have the time to do it like this, but maybe you could try it as a special thing from time to time. It's so simple – just flour and water, and yeast – but it's something you almost nurture and then you watch it grow. I love it.

I have included Daniel's recipe for his *pagnotta* loaf on page 155, for which he uses four different grains. It's a very rustic, heavy, dark bread that is beautiful and chewy to eat. Then there's pizza with gorgonzola and a little tomato (*see* page 154); we lay prosciutto on it when it comes out of the oven and the heat from the pizza warms it up and the prosciutto almost melts into the crust. It's sensual and flavoursome, and when you eat it you're biting through clean prosciutto that hasn't dried up and gone hard. I've also included a focaccia with rosemary and Parmigiano-Reggiano (*see* page 156), and a schiacciata (page 156), which is an interesting savoury–sweet bread with grapes pushed into it.

*The variety of pizza toppings is endless, limited only by your imagination and the season. I like simple toppings – less is definitely more when it comes to pizza. Don't be tempted to overload. This is one of my family's all-time favourites.*

# Pizza al prosciutto e gorgonzola

## PIZZA WITH PROSCIUTTO AND GORGONZOLA

olive oil

flour

1 quantity Pizza Dough
 (*see* page 21)

200 ml Tomato Sauce
 (*see* page 18)

200 g mozzarella, thinly sliced

100 g gorgonzola, broken into small pieces

sea salt

freshly ground black pepper

1 tablespoon freshly chopped parsley

200 g prosciutto, sliced

handful of rocket

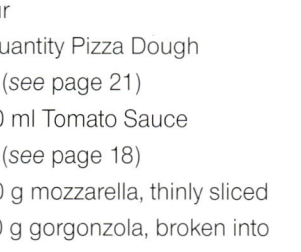 Preheat the oven to 200°C. Lightly but thoroughly oil a pizza tray. Flour your work surface and tip the dough onto it. Using your hands, work the dough into a smooth ball, bringing the sides in towards the bottom. Put it onto the pizza tray and cover with a clean tea towel, then rest in a warm area for 15 minutes until doubled in size.

Press the ball of dough down from the top, stretching it out to cover the pizza tray. It should be no more than 1 cm thick. Spread with a thin layer of tomato sauce. Cover with the mozzarella slices, then scatter over the gorgonzola pieces. Season with salt and pepper and sprinkle with the parsley. Bake for 12–15 minutes or until the bottom is golden brown.

Remove from the oven and immediately lay the prosciutto slices on and scatter the rocket on top. Serve immediately.

*In Puglia the dense, chewy bread is known as* pagnotta, *and it is the best thing for sauces and soups. On occasion I have been caught dipping* pagnotta *in red wine to eat as a snack! In the restaurant we use Daniel Di Chirico's bread, and this is his recipe.*

# Pagnotta

Combine the yeast and warm water in a large bowl, then set aside for about 10 minutes until they froth. Add the water and *biga* and, using an electric mixer fitted with a paddle, blend well. Add the flour and salt and mix for 1–2 minutes until the dough comes together and pulls away from the sides of the bowl (you may need to add a little more flour). Replace the paddle with a dough hook, then knead on a medium speed for 3–5 minutes until soft and elastic. With floured hands, knead on a floured surface for about 1 minute until the dough loses its stickiness and is velvety. Put into a lightly oiled large bowl and cover with plastic wrap. Leave for about 3 hours until tripled in size. Do not punch down.

Line 1–2 baking trays with baking paper and scatter with flour. Generously flour your work surface and have more flour nearby for your hands. Tip the dough onto your work surface and flour the top, then cut into 2 or 3 equal-sized pieces (to make 2 large loaves or 3 smaller loaves). Flatten each piece and roll it up lengthwise, using your thumbs as a guide. Turn each piece 90 degrees and pat it flat, then roll up again. Roll each piece into a ball, then, using your work surface to generate tension, pull the dough taut across the top. Transfer to the trays and cover with a heavy cloth. Leave in a draught-free place for about 1 hour until doubled in size.

Preheat the oven to 220°C 30 minutes before baking. Transfer the loaves to your work surface 5–10 minutes before baking. Flour the tops and, using your fingertips, dimple them all over (the imprints will disappear, but will keep the bread from rising too much in the oven). Let stand for 5–10 minutes. Meanwhile, remove and discard the baking paper and sprinkle the baking trays with semolina. Slide the loaves onto the baking trays and bake until golden brown and crusty (50–60 minutes if making 2 loaves and 30–35 minutes for 3 loaves). Knock on the bottom of each loaf – if you hear a hollow ring, it is cooked through. Cool on wire racks.

*Makes 2–3*

9 g fresh yeast
¼ cup warm water
3 cups water
200 g Biga (*see* page 22)
1.125 kg unbleached flour
1 tablespoon salt
olive oil
semolina

*This savoury–sweet bread is delicious as a snack just on its own with a coffee, but it also works well with the savoury part of a meal in place of bread. The sweetness of the grapes popping in your mouth every now and then is sensational.*

## Schiacciata all'uva

### SCHIACCIATA WITH GRAPES

olive oil
1 quantity Pizza Dough
 (*see* page 21)
300 g dark-coloured grapes
 (muscatels are good)
sea salt

Preheat the oven to 180°C. Grease a 30 cm round cake tin well with olive oil. Press the dough into it evenly. Pick the grapes from their stems and press the grapes into the dough, pushing down and making indentations. Ensure that the dough is well covered with grapes. Season with salt and drizzle with oil, then allow to rest for 10 minutes. Bake for 15–20 minutes or until the bottom of the dough is golden brown. Serve hot, warm or cold.

*The best time to make focaccia is when you are making pizza – so that you can make use of the oven.*

## Focaccia al rosmarino

### FOCACCIA WITH ROSEMARY

1 quantity Pizza Dough
 (*see* page 21)
1 clove garlic, crushed
2½ tablespoons olive oil
5 sprigs rosemary
100 g freshly grated Parmigiano-
 Reggiano
sea salt

Preheat the oven to 180°C. Grease a 30 cm round cake tin well with olive oil. Press the dough into it evenly (to a thickness of about 3 cm). Combine the garlic and oil, then spread it over the dough, pressing down with your fingers as you go to make many indentations. Break up the rosemary sprigs and scatter over the dough. Press the rosemary in with your fingers, then sprinkle over the Parmigiano-Reggiano and season with salt. Allow to rest for 10 minutes. Bake for 15–20 minutes or until the bottom is golden and well cooked. It should sound hollow when tapped. Serve hot, warm or cold.

*Opposite: Schiacciata all'uva (bottom) and Focaccia al Rosmarino (top)*

*This wonderful sweet bread comes from Firenze (Florence), where it is baked during the festa of San Lorenzo. I like to make it at Christmas as an alternative to panettone.*

# Pan di San Lorenzo

750 g flour
pinch of salt
60 g butter
½ cup currants
½ cup sultanas
½ cup raisins
1 teaspoon mixed spice
60 g fresh yeast
2 cups tepid water
½ cup sugar
2 teaspoons powdered milk

### Glaze (optional)
½ cup sugar
¼ cup water
1 teaspoon powdered gelatine

Sift the flour and salt into a large bowl, then rub in the butter until the mixture resembles breadcrumbs. Stir in the dried fruit and mixed spice. In a separate bowl, combine the yeast with half the water and set aside until it froths. In another bowl, combine the sugar and powdered milk with the remaining water. Stir the milk mixture into the flour mixture, then add the yeast mixture and stir until a soft dough forms. Turn the dough out onto a floured surface and knead until soft and elastic. Transfer to a large, clean bowl and cover with a tea towel. Set aside in a warm place for 30 minutes–1 hour until the dough has almost doubled in size.

Turn the dough out onto a floured surface and knead again for a couple of minutes. Shape into a large loaf, or divide into 16 pieces and shape into buns. Cover again and set aside for 30 minutes–1 hour in a warm place until doubled in size.

Preheat the oven to 180°C. Transfer the dough to a baking tray and bake for 25 minutes until golden brown and the top springs back when touched lightly. If desired, glaze the bread – combine all ingredients and brush the top of the loaf while it is still warm. Serve warm or cold.   *Makes 1 large loaf or 16 buns*

These classic little bites and nibbles don't necessarily fit within a traditional meal, but can be enjoyed *intermezzo*, or 'in the middle', as a forerunner to dining or as a beautiful snack married with a Campari at the bar. Maybe it's mid-afternoon and you need a little something with an espresso. Maybe you missed lunch, or dinner's going to be late. Or perhaps it's after dinner, and you want something simple to enjoy with a glass of wine. These in-between dishes have been created to *ingannare lo stomaco*, that is, 'to cheat the stomach'.

It wasn't until one time when I was in Venice that I truly understood the perfection of these tasty morsels. On foot one day, with lunch not long finished and dinner still a way off, we passed *un caffè* and couldn't help but go in. The bar was laden with small white-bread sandwiches filled with tuna and mayonnaise, known locally as *tartine* (*see* page 167). These little sandwiches (or *tramezzetti* as I know them, which means 'for in-between') are very common in Italian bars, cut very small and filled with crab, chicken or tuna. You might be having a refreshing beer on a warm afternoon, and you don't really need to eat, so you have a few of these.

I remember reading that Arrigo Cipriani, who runs the famous Harry's Bar in Venice, was asked by an American journalist what he put in Harry's renowned chicken and mayonnaise sandwiches to make them so special. Arrigo said, 'Chicken and mayonnaise.' Apparently the reporter thought he was hiding something and got irritated and pressed him about it. Arrigo said, 'To be honest, there is something

I didn't tell you that we put in – it's a bit of love.' He meant that someone takes care with them and makes sure all the ingredients are right. These little snippets don't lack substance – there's a lot of tradition in the way they're prepared, and they still need high-quality ingredients.

There's a huge variety of *stuzzichini*, or appetisers, in the Italian repertoire, that rally the tastebuds and prepare them for the meal to come. You might try *baccalà* balls (*see* page 164), the salted-cod balls that are very popular in northern Italy, especially around Easter. They have an intense burst of salty flavour. The same is true of the pastries with anchovy paste (page 167). These require you to order a beer! You want another, and then another. Of course, you can only eat so much, because your palate just explodes. With these kinds of dishes, the principles can be kept while interchanging the ingredients, the toppings and fillings. You can enjoy the savoury *crostini* (page 170) with olive paste, or maybe with sun-dried tomato paste, roasted capsicum or chicken liver pâté.

I believe these in-betweens perfectly blend the cultural aspects of food and wine in an informal setting (which also makes them ideal for a cocktail party). They fit a mood of fun, conversation and frivolity, and what I like most is the tactile quality of eating them with your fingers – a most decadent experience.

*When you taste the sweetness of this Veneto-inspired pie, you will want more. It looks sensational and makes an ideal snack when served at room temperature. The pastry can be used for lots of other things – when I have offcuts I roll them out and bake them as savoury biscotti.*

1½ cups flour
1 teaspoon salt
2 teaspoons freshly chopped sage
2 teaspoons freshly chopped rosemary
100 g softened unsalted butter
⅓ cup water

*Pumpkin filling*
1.5 kg pumpkin, peeled and cut into small pieces
sea salt
freshly ground black pepper
olive oil
1 leek (white part only), finely chopped and well washed
1 cup freshly grated Parmigiano-Reggiano
1 cup freshly grated gruyère cheese
2 eggs
1 tablespoon softened butter

# Torta di zucca

## PUMPKIN PIE

Sift the flour into a large bowl, then add the salt, herbs and butter. Using your fingertips, rub the butter into the flour until it resembles breadcrumbs. Add the water and mix until a dough forms. Form the dough into a ball and wrap it in plastic wrap. Refrigerate for at least 1 hour – ideally, overnight.

Preheat the oven to 180°C. Put the pumpkin into an oven tray and season with salt and pepper. Bake for 15 minutes or until cooked through. Set aside to cool. Meanwhile, heat a little olive oil in a frying pan, then add the leek and sauté gently until golden.

Transfer the cooked pumpkin to a food processor and blend until just smooth. Add the leek, cheeses, eggs and butter and taste for salt and pepper.

Roll out the dough to a thickness of 1 cm, then use half of it to line a 20 cm pie dish. Fill with the pumpkin mixture, then cover with the remaining pastry. Bake for 30–40 minutes until golden. Serve hot, warm or cold.

Baccalà, *or salted cod, is very popular in the north of Italy, where they started doing it many years ago to preserve their fish. I love it. Several different dishes from Venice and Verona use it. My mum is from Verona, so we had it a lot when I was growing up, especially around Easter time. We'd braise it in the oven with tomato and onions and capers. You need to soak* baccalà *in water for several days in advance – if you don't soak it for long enough it can be inedible because of the salt. These* baccalà *balls are an intense flavour burst. I can eat half a dozen, but for some people they are too salty to have that many.*

# Crocchette di baccalà

### FRIED BACCALÀ BALLS

1 side of baccalà,
    cut into 2.5 cm strips
1 tablespoon olive oil
1 onion, finely chopped
2 cloves garlic, sliced
2 potatoes, roughly chopped
dash of dry white wine
1 cup freshly chopped
    flat-leaf parsley
pinch of freshly ground
    black pepper
2 cups cream
1 tablespoon extra-virgin
    olive oil
dash of verjuice
3 eggs
flour
3 cups dried breadcrumbs
1 litre olive oil for frying

 Soak the *baccalà* in fresh, cold water for 2–3 days, changing the water 5–6 times.

Heat the olive oil in a heavy-based pot, then add the onion and garlic. Sauté over a medium heat until the onion is soft, then add the *baccalà* and potato. Toss well. Pour in the wine, then add the parsley, pepper and cream and cook over a low heat for 20 minutes. Remove from the heat and allow to cool. Purée in a food processor, drizzling in the extra-virgin olive oil until a paste is formed. Add the verjuice. Blend in 1 of the eggs – the mixture should be quite firm. Form into golfball-sized balls, then dust with flour and shake off the excess.

Lightly beat the remaining eggs. Dip the *baccalà* balls into the beaten egg, then coat with breadcrumbs. Heat the litre of oil to about 180°C in a large pot or a deep-fryer. Fry the *baccalà* balls in batches for 3–4 minutes until golden, gently moving them around to ensure they are evenly coloured. Remove with a slotted spoon and drain on kitchen paper. Serve immediately.    *Makes 12*

*Once, in the kitchen, Chris and I were fiddling around with some leftover pastry. Usually we would have made something sweet, but this time we decided to put some anchovies through it. We rolled it out and baked the pastries, and they had a wonderful burst of savoury saltiness.*

## Sfoglia all'acciuga

### ANCHOVY PASTRIES

olive oil
flour
250 g Puff Pastry
　(see page 22)
50 g anchovy fillets
1 tablespoon paprika

Preheat the oven to 200°C and grease a baking tray with olive oil. Flour your workbench, then roll out the puff pastry to form a rectangular sheet 5 mm thick. Break up the anchovies and distribute them over the pastry. Starting with the long edge, roll the sheet into a cylinder, then cut the filled pastry into 10 × 1 cm thick slices. Lay the slices on the floured workbench and roll them to a thickness of 3 mm. Put on a greased baking sheet and bake for 15–20 minutes or until golden brown. Sprinkle with the paprika and serve immediately.   *Makes 10*

*Nothing could be simpler than these* tartine, *which are available as afternoon snacks in bars throughout Italy. They are perfect to drink with. Use the best tuna you can get – it's worth it. I like Ortiz, a Spanish brand.*

butter
8 slices fresh white bread
1 × 200 g can best-quality tuna
½ red onion, finely chopped
2½ tablespoons Mayonnaise
　(see page 18)
1 tablespoon freshly chopped
　flat-leaf parsley
sea salt
freshly ground black pepper

## Tramezzetti con tonno

### TUNA SANDWICHES

Butter the bread and set aside. Combine the tuna, onion, mayonnaise and parsley in a bowl. Season to taste with salt and pepper and mix well. Put the tuna mixture between 2 slices of bread to form sandwiches. Traditionally the crusts are cut off, but this is optional. Cut each sandwich into 4 fingers to serve.   *Makes 16*

Opposite: *Sfoglia all'acciuga*

*The best time to make these delightful snacky treats is when there is some leftover risotto or ragù lying about the place – but they're worth making from scratch, too! The word suppli is Roman dialect for rice croquettes. The very popular* suppli al telefono *have a piece of mozzarella in the middle instead of meat ragù, and when you bite in the cheese stretches to resemble telephone wires, hence the name of the dish.*

olive oil
60 g butter
1 small onion, diced
2 cups arborio rice
1 litre Chicken Stock
    (*see* page 20)
pinch of saffron *or* to taste
sea salt
freshly ground black pepper
80 g freshly grated Parmigiano-
    Reggiano
flour
3 eggs, lightly beaten
3 cups dried breadcrumbs

*Veal ragù*
50 ml olive oil
1 onion, chopped
1 clove garlic, finely chopped
1 carrot, diced
1 stick celery, diced
200 g minced veal
sea salt
freshly ground black pepper
4 tablespoons tomato paste
100 ml red wine
400 ml Chicken Stock
    (*see* page 20)

# Suppli di riso al ragù

## RICE BALLS FILLED WITH VEAL RAGÙ

Heat a dash of olive oil and half the butter in a heavy-based pot and fry the onion over a medium heat until translucent. Add the rice and sauté for 1–2 minutes, then pour in the chicken stock. Add the saffron and season to taste with salt and pepper. Reduce the heat and simmer, covered, for about 20 minutes until the rice is cooked, stirring from time to time. Stir in the Parmigiano-Reggiano and the remaining butter until well combined. Pour the mixture into a shallow dish and set aside to cool.

To make the veal ragù, heat the olive oil and fry the onion and garlic over a medium heat until translucent. Add the carrot and celery and fry until soft. Stir in the veal and brown well. Taste for salt and pepper, then add the tomato paste and stir for a few minutes. Pour in the wine. Simmer for 2–3 minutes, then add the stock. Reduce the heat slightly and cook gently for 45 minutes, stirring occasionally. The ragù should be quite thick. Remove from the heat and allow to cool.

Take a large spoonful of the rice mixture and roll it in the palm of your hand to form a ball. Push a hole in one side and fill with a spoonful of the ragù. Roll again to seal the hole, ensuring the ragù is completely enclosed. Repeat with the remaining rice mixture and ragù. Heat 50 ml olive oil in a large pot or a deep-fryer until very hot. Roll each rice ball in flour, then egg, then breadcrumbs and fry in batches for about 4 minutes until golden. Drain on kitchen paper. Serve immediately.   *Makes 10–12*

*The endless range of toppings for crostini (toasted bread) are traditionally influenced by region and season. For example, in southern Italy a tuna and white bean topping is popular. This rich duck-liver topping has a Tuscan heritage.*

1 breadstick,
    cut into 20 × 5 mm slices
100 ml olive oil
2 shallots *or*
    1 small onion, diced
1 clove garlic, finely chopped
300 g duck livers,
    trimmed and chopped
50 g speck *or* pancetta,
    finely chopped
1 tablespoon flour
½ cup Marsala
½ cup white wine
1 cup Demi-glace
    (see page 19)
1 tablespoon freshly chopped
    sage
1 tablespoon freshly chopped
    flat-leaf parsley
sea salt
freshly ground black pepper

# Crostini fegatini

## CROSTINI WITH DUCK-LIVER RAGÙ

Preheat the oven to 180°C or the griller to moderate. Toast the bread in the oven or under the griller for a few minutes on both sides until golden, then arrange on a serving platter and set aside.

Heat the olive oil in a deep pot and add the shallots and garlic. Sauté over a medium heat until translucent, then add the liver and speck and sauté for 4–5 minutes until golden brown, stirring to prevent sticking. Add the flour and mix well. Stir in the Marsala and wine, then add the meat glaze, the sage and half the parsley and toss. Bring to the boil, then reduce the heat and season with salt and pepper. Simmer for 20 minutes, stirring occasionally.

Top each *crostini* with a generous spoonful of the liver ragù. Sprinkle with the remaining parsley and serve.   *Makes 20*

# Sweet Things

The lovely treats in this chapter are from the part of the menu that's more for indulgence than for nourishment. You don't really need them, so they're a bit naughty!

It's tempting to tuck in and enjoy something small and sweet with a coffee in the afternoon, perhaps in a typical *piazza* with a couple of old men playing cards outside the coffee shop with a dog next to them and bikes riding past, and the smell of buttery biscuits being baked. It's a tradition that's been transported from Italian cities around the world, and you can see it when you take a walk down Melbourne's streets, where there are shops with windows full of beautiful pastries and cakes.

Italians make small sweet delights not only for dessert, but for any time. Some of the following are sweets you can enjoy at any time of the day, such as little *bomboloni* doughnuts (*see* page 176). A few of them we grew up with as children, like the *crostoli* Mum always made for us (page 179). These simple, fried pastries, sprinkled with icing sugar, are very moreish. They're so wonderful and light that if you have one with an espresso, you reach for another one without thinking. I remember always having them around the house, especially on festive occasions – Mum would cook up a large batch at Easter and Christmas. It's great to serve them in a big stack – they look beautifully rustic, with an understated, handcrafted elegance.

Naturally, I've included some great plated desserts here as well, to complete a meal. One of the things I love about Italian-style desserts is that they look really good when served, without having to be perfect and pristine. At home we do our *semifreddo* in a big bowl; it doesn't look prissy or refined, and everybody loves tucking into it. Once you get a taste for it, you just forget the diet and go for more! I love desserts like this, that look handmade – they have such character. It's like when you've been to your grandma or auntie's place and a cake has just come out of the oven – it may not look like the most perfect cake in the world, but there's a lot of love in it and it looks handcrafted. There's something really special about that feeling, and I like to think the sweet things in this book reflect that.

I'm one of those who have been a bit fearful of desserts in the past, because they're more 'scientific' in the preparation. You have to take the time and effort to measure quantities more carefully. Recipes have to be adhered to more closely – you can't just get stuck in and start cutting things up and throwing them together. But once you understand the techniques and get a feel for a few of the basic recipes, you can start to make substitutions confidently and experiment a bit more. For example, there's no reason why the beautiful quince and almond tart on page 188 can't become a beautiful peach and almond tart during the summer weather. With practice you also learn that the way you put butter, flour, sugar and eggs together in a basic cake recipe determines what the cake will be like. More of one ingredient will make it heavier, perhaps richer, and less of that ingredient will tend to make it lighter. Once you've grasped this, you can decide that you love a cake but would like it to be a bit lighter, so you try it with a little less flour. I think that's exciting, because you start to develop your own recipes and put your own personality into them.

In this chapter I've included recipes that demonstrate a variety of techniques. There's some baking, such as with the Monte Bianco flourless chocolate cake with a white chestnut cream (see page 199), and working with gelatine or aspic in the delicate buttermilk *pannacotta* (page 191). The buttermilk adds a bit of sourness, so it's a refreshing dessert. Working with heated sugar is another technique, which I've covered with the *semifreddo* (page 193). The texture of the finished dish depends on the sugar being cooked to a certain temperature so that it doesn't set in the freezer. To keep it soft and pliable, but not runny, you have to get the recipe right – an example of needing to be a bit more rigid.

Part of the whole Italian philosophy of food is that we love to hold on to our traditions and make sure the basics are intact, but we also don't ignore what's happening around us. So we try to develop new things, like the buttermilk *pannacotta* or the saffron pears (see page 179). Saffron is not often associated with dessert. I love it in savoury dishes such as risotto, but I think it has a real place in sweet dishes, too. It's quite rich, but you only need a few strands, and it imparts an amazing colour. It's interesting to fiddle around with savoury or sweet flavours, trying to interchange things a bit. Sometimes the results are very surprising! I've included a recipe for rice pudding, because I don't think rice gets enough of a look-in for sweet dishes. One of my good friends, Gabriel Turon, owns a very famous rice mill in Italy and loves to demonstrate desserts made with rice, including a rice *gelato* that is absolutely magnificent.

But we also love the traditional and regional favourites, so I've included a very typical *cassata alla siciliana* (see page 180), which I've taken right back to how it was originally intended to be made. The *cassata* recipe is a really old one that has changed over the years, but I've made it as traditional as I can, and I think it's really nice to bring things back like that. You tend to forget how things started when you see different commercial versions – often they're not what they were meant to be in the first place.

*Cantuccini or biscotti di Prato are as Tuscan as the Palio di Siena. They're perfect for the Italian habit of dunking. Tuscans, in particular, love to dunk things in their coffee and in their vin santo ('wine of the saints'), an aged dessert wine. Almond cakes or biscotti seem to be the perfect partner for vin santo.*

# Cantuccini

## ALMOND BISCUITS

Preheat the oven to 180°C. Put the almonds on a baking tray and bake for 8–10 minutes or until golden brown. Allow to cool, then chop into slivers. Reduce the oven to 160°C.

Lightly grease and flour a large baking tray. Combine 2 cups flour, the sugar and the baking soda in a large bowl. In a separate bowl, whisk the eggs, vanilla extract and almond extract until fluffy. Add the egg mixture to the dry ingredients and mix until the dough just clings together. Fold in the almonds and cherries. Divide the dough in half and roll each piece into a 30 cm × 3 cm log (about 2 cm high). Put the logs onto the baking tray at least 5 cm apart. Bake for 45 minutes or until light golden. They should be firm to the touch.

Transfer the logs to a wire rack and allow to cool for 5 minutes. Holding a sharp serrated knife at a 45-degree angle, cut the logs into 1 cm slices. Serve immediately if you like your biscuits to have a slightly softer, moist centre, or put them back onto the baking tray and return to the oven for 10 minutes to make them even crispier. The biscuits will keep for 3–4 days if stored in an airtight container. *Makes about 36*

½ cup blanched almonds
butter (for greasing)
2 cups unbleached *or* white plain flour
¾ cup sugar
1 teaspoon baking soda
3 eggs
1 teaspoon vanilla extract
¼ teaspoon almond extract
½ cup glacé cherries, chopped

*These sweets could easily have gone into the 'Intermezzo' chapter, because you can have them any time. For me, they're an afternoon fix! When I smell good coffee brewing, I immediately think of having one of these with it. Bomboloni should be light, not stodgy. They can be filled with all kinds of things, but I prefer pastry cream, as the Siciliani make them. I love serving up a big pile and letting people help themselves.*

# Bomboloni

## ITALIAN DOUGHNUTS FILLED WITH PASTRY CREAM

2 teaspoons fresh yeast
warm water
1 kg plain flour
   (preferably Italian type '00')
1 tablespoon salt
2½ cups caster sugar
zest of 1 orange, finely chopped
10 eggs
400 g softened unsalted butter
2 large pinches cinnamon
2 cups vegetable oil
200 g jam *or* Pastry Cream
   (*see* page 24)

Put the yeast into a cup and squash with a little warm water, then set aside until it froths. Combine the flour, salt and 100 g of the sugar in a bowl, then add the orange zest. In a separate bowl, whisk the eggs and yeast. Add the egg mixture to the flour mixture and mix in an electric mixer until the dough comes away from the sides of the bowl. If it is too stiff, add a drop of cold water. Mix in the butter until it is evenly incorporated and the dough is glossy and smooth. Cover the bowl with plastic wrap and allow to rest for 30 minutes–1 hour until the dough has doubled in size. Knock back the dough, then wrap it in plastic wrap and refrigerate for 2 hours.

Put the dough on a floured work surface and roll it into balls about 5 cm in height. Put the balls on a tray and cover with a clean tea towel. Allow to rest for 45 minutes–1 hour until tripled in size.

Mix the remaining sugar and the cinnamon and spread on a tray. Heat the vegetable oil in a large pot or a deep-fryer until hot. Fry the *bomboloni* in batches for a few minutes until they are golden brown. Lift from the oil using a slotted spoon and roll immediately in the cinnamon sugar. Using a piping bag, fill the bomboloni with jam or pastry cream while still warm.   *Makes about 20*

*One of Mum's favourite things is to cook brown pears in sugar. She ends up with sticky caramelised fruit, with a gooey texture on the outside and a fresh, cleansing pear sensation inside. I've taken that idea and added saffron to it.*

# Pere al zafferano

SAFFRON HONEY PEARS

Peel each pear and remove its base. Using a melon baller, remove the bottom half of each core. Put the saffron into a heavy-based pot over a medium heat. Toast for about 2 minutes, then remove the pot from the heat. Stand the pears in the pot, then add the sugar and honey. Pour in enough water to just cover the pears. Return the pot to the heat and bring to the boil. Reduce the heat and simmer for 15 minutes until the pears are tender and a rich gold colour.

Using a slotted spoon, lift the pears from the liquid and put into a large dish. Increase the heat to medium and reduce the cooking liquid until syrupy. Pour the syrup over the pears, then allow to cool. Serve with double cream, crème fraîche or ice-cream.   *Serves 6*

6 brown pears
    (preferably winter nelis)
2 teaspoons saffron threads
250 g sugar
½ cup honey
water

*These sweet, fried treats have been cooked in my family for many, many years.*

# Crostoli

Whisk the eggs and half the icing sugar until thick and creamy. Add the flour, vanilla extract and Marsala. Using an electric mixer fitted with a dough hook, knead for 15 minutes until the dough is elastic. Cut into 4 equal parts and, using a pasta machine, roll out each portion until smooth and silky and about 2 mm thick. Using a crinkle cutter, cut into ribbons about 2 cm wide. Place on a floured tray. Heat the oil in a large pot or a deep-fryer until hot. Deep fry the *crostoli* in batches for 2 minutes, moving them around in the oil, until golden brown. Drain on kitchen paper and allow to cool. Pile the *crostoli* on a plate and dust with the remaining icing sugar to serve. They will stay light and crisp for days if stored in an airtight container.   *Makes 30–40*

5 eggs
2 cups icing sugar
600 g flour
1 teaspoon vanilla extract
150 ml Marsala
2 litres vegetable oil

*Opposite:* Pere al Zafferano

*Cassata comes from the word* cassa, *which means 'box' or 'case'. It's a moulded dessert from Sicily, in which the mould is lined with sponge soaked in sugar and* alchermes, *a red Italian liqueur used specifically for cooking. The cassata sets and is turned out with a lovely orange glaze. Sicily always reminds me of warm European weather and beautiful blood oranges.*

# Cassata alla siciliana

1 kg ricotta, well drained
5 tablespoons caster sugar
5 tablespoons icing sugar
½ cup candied orange rind,
    cut into small pieces
½ cup candied citron,
    cut into small pieces
½ cup bittersweet chocolate,
    cut into small pieces
2 tablespoons maraschino liqueur
2 cups water
½ cup sugar
2 teaspoons freshly squeezed
    orange juice, strained
2 tablespoons alchermes liqueur

*Sponge cake*
5 eggs
¼ cup sugar
½ cup flour
½ cup cornflour
30 g butter, melted and cooled

*Orange glaze*
zest of 2 oranges,
    cut into fine strips
2 cups freshly squeezed
    orange juice, strained
2 cups sugar

Mix the ricotta with the caster sugar, icing sugar, candied orange rind, candied citron and chocolate. Add half the *maraschino* and stir well, then cover and refrigerate for at least 3 hours.

To make the sponge cake, preheat the oven to 180°C. Butter and flour a 24 cm springform cake tin. Using an electric mixer, whisk the eggs and sugar for 15 minutes until thick and fluffy. Combine the flour and cornflour and sift 3 times. Gently fold the flour mixture into the egg mixture a little at a time. When all the flour has been incorporated, fold in the melted butter. Pour into the prepared tin and bake for 25–30 minutes until golden and springy to the touch and a skewer inserted comes out clean. Allow to cool for a few minutes in the tin, then turn out onto a wire rack and cool completely.

Combine the water, sugar and orange juice in a medium saucepan and bring to the boil. Reduce the heat to medium and simmer for 15 minutes. Cut the sponge cake into 3 cm triangular slices and use to line the sides and bottom of a large glass or ceramic bowl, setting aside enough cake to cover the top of the *cassata*. Add the remaining *maraschino* and the *alchermes* to the sugar syrup, then pour some of the syrup gently over the sponge lining. Transfer the ricotta mixture to the mould and smooth the top. Cover with the reserved sponge cake to enclose the filling. Sprinkle with the remaining syrup. Refrigerate the *cassata* for at least 3 hours before serving.

To make the orange glaze, combine the zest, juice and sugar in a heavy-based saucepan and bring to the boil over a high heat. Reduce the heat and simmer for about 30 minutes, stirring occasionally. Allow to cool completely before serving.

To serve, turn the *cassata* out onto a serving platter. Drench with orange glaze, then cut into wedges.   *Serves 8*

*This beautiful dish came to me by accident, from a colleague somewhere along the line who was visiting and needed the use of an ice-cream machine. He used our restaurant machine and left the recipe behind, saying, 'Give this a go – you'll love it.' We've used it ever since, but I can't give him credit because, sadly, I can't remember who he was! The recipe uses a large number of egg yolks, which yield a rich and luscious ice-cream.*

# Terrina di gelato alle spezie con pane alle spezie e sciroppo di vino

## SPICED ICE-CREAM TERRINE WITH SPICED BREAD AND RED-WINE SYRUP

*Cinnamon ice-cream*

1 cup Sugar Syrup
  (see page 23)
1 tablespoon ground cinnamon
16 egg yolks
250 ml cream,
  lightly whipped

*Saffron ice-cream*

1 cup Sugar Syrup
  (see page 23)
1 tablespoon saffron threads
16 egg yolks
250 ml cream, lightly whipped

*Star anise ice-cream*

1 cup Sugar Syrup
  (see page 23)
1 tablespoon ground star anise
16 egg yolks
250 ml cream, lightly whipped

To make the cinnamon ice-cream, combine the sugar syrup and cinnamon in a small saucepan. Bring to the boil, then reduce the heat and simmer for 10 minutes. Transfer to a large stainless steel bowl and allow to cool a little. Set the bowl over a saucepan or bowl of hot water and whisk for 10–15 minutes until thick and glossy. Allow to cool. Fold in the cream, then churn in an ice-cream machine according to the manufacturer's instructions.

Make the saffron ice-cream and the star anise ice-cream following the same method.

Line a 2 litre terrine mould with greaseproof paper. Spoon in the anise ice-cream and smooth it with the back of a large spoon to flatten the layer as much as possible. Freeze for 30 minutes, then repeat with the saffron ice-cream. Freeze again for 30 minutes, then top with the cinnamon ice-cream. Return the terrine to the freezer. (It will keep for at least 2 weeks.) ▶

*Spiced bread*
250 g Italian chestnut-flower honey *or* other honey
125 g strong rye flour
125 g plain flour
1 tablespoon baking powder
½ cup milk
3 eggs
50 g sugar
1 teaspoon ground cinnamon
pinch of ground anise
2 drops vanilla extract

*Red-wine syrup*
1 cup red wine
250 g sugar

To make the spiced bread, preheat the oven to 150°C and line a loaf tin with greaseproof paper. Gently heat the honey in a saucepan for a few minutes until runny, then allow to cool slightly. Sift the flours and baking powder into a large bowl. Pour in the honey and mix to a smooth paste. Add the milk, eggs and sugar and whisk until smooth and creamy. Add the spices and vanilla extract and mix until a smooth dough forms. Transfer to the prepared tin and bake for 1 hour until an inserted skewer comes out clean. Allow to cool completely before serving. (The bread will keep for 1 week in the refrigerator, or longer if frozen.)

To make the red-wine syrup, combine the wine and sugar in a heavy-based saucepan. Bring to the boil, then reduce heat to moderate and allow to reduce by half. Allow to cool completely. (The syrup will keep for at least a year stored in a cool place.)

To serve, cut the spiced bread and the ice-cream into 1 cm thick slices. Serve a slice of bread alongside a slice of ice-cream, or sit the ice-cream on top of the bread. Drizzle with red-wine syrup. *Serves 15–20*

*I know I always talk about eating together and sharing, but with desserts I think that occasionally putting out something individual can make it feel more special. This elegant, glossy fig tart is a good example. It's a perfect fit for winter or autumn. The spiced red wine resembles the Veneto region's* vin brule, *making this a Northern Italian dish.*

# Torta di fichi

## FIG TART

500 g flour
170 g icing sugar
250 g softened butter
¼ cup milk
2 eggs
2 cups red wine
1 cinnamon stick
1 star anise
¼ teaspoon white pepper
1 vanilla bean, split
500 g sugar
1 cup water
12 ripe figs
1 cup Pastry Cream
   (*see* page 24), warmed

Combine the flour and icing sugar in a large bowl. Using the tips of your fingers, rub in the butter until the mixture resembles breadcrumbs. Add the milk and eggs and mix until a firm dough forms. Refrigerate for 1 hour.

Put the red wine, cinnamon, star anise, pepper, vanilla bean, sugar and water into a heavy-based saucepan. Cook over a moderate heat until the liquid is reduced and syrupy. Add the whole figs and reduce the heat to low. Cook for 5 minutes until the figs have softened, then remove from the heat and allow to cool.

Preheat the oven to 180°C and grease a large, deep loose-bottomed flan tin (or 4 × 9 cm tins) with a little butter. Roll out the dough to a thickness of 5 mm, then line the prepared tin with it. Line with aluminium foil and fill with dried beans, then bake for 10 minutes. Remove the beans. Pour the warmed pastry cream into the tart case and arrange the figs on top. Drizzle the syrup over and serve warm or cold.

*Once you've got your components set up for these pastries – puff pastry bases, poached apples, frangipane – the finished product is only minutes away. I love a dessert like this. Sometimes the easier it is to make, the more impressive it can look.*

# Tortine di mele

## CARAMEL APPLE PASTRIES

5 Granny Smith apples, peeled
2 cups water
500 g sugar
500 g Puff Pastry (see page 22)
200 g Frangipane (see page 24)
1 egg, lightly beaten
dash of milk

*Caramel apple sauce*
200 g sugar
175 ml water
poached apple (see method)

Peel the apples and cut the cheeks away from the core. Put the water and sugar into a pot and bring to the boil, then reduce the heat to a simmer. Add the apple, cover and cook for 15 minutes or until the apple is tender but still holding its shape. Set aside the best-looking pieces for the apple pastries and use the remainder for the sauce. Reserve the poaching liquid and keep warm.

To make the caramel apple sauce, combine the sugar and 75 ml of the water in a heavy-based saucepan. Bring to the boil, then cook for 10 minutes until golden. Remove from the heat and quickly but carefully add the remaining water. Return to the heat and cook briefly until any solid bits in the caramel have melted. Stir in the reserved poached apple and set aside.

Preheat the oven to 200°C and line a baking tray with baking paper. Roll out the puff pastry to a thickness of about 5 mm, then cut out 24 circles 8.5 cm in diameter. Using a 5 cm diameter cutter, cut out the centre from 12 of the circles. Mix the milk into the beaten egg, brush each solid disc with egg wash and put a holed disc on top. Fill the hole with the frangipane and refrigerate for 10 minutes. Top the frangipane with a piece of poached apple, then brush with the reserved poaching liquid and sprinkle with sugar. Put the pastries on the prepared tray and bake for about 12 minutes or until golden. Drizzle generously with the caramel apple sauce and serve immediately.   *Makes 12*

Note: With this simple recipe you can be prepared way ahead of time, even having the pastry bases set up with bits on them in the freezer. You won't have to spend any time away from your guests at all. Just walk into the kitchen, pop the pastries into the oven and 12 minutes later, there they are, ready to serve. *Ecco!*

*I have a fascination with quinces. They always make you think of winter, but when you have them preserved, you can use them any time. With their amazing texture and flavour, they work with savoury dishes as well as desserts. When I'm roasting quinces in syrup with a little brandy before bottling them, I love to take out a few and put them into a big bowl, then send them into the dining room and say, 'Who wants some roasted quince with a blob of clotted cream?' They're so natural and real, and it's a lovely way to eat them. The pastry in this recipe has a lovely sweetness. You can use it for other desserts as well.*

225 g plain flour
1 tablespoon cornflour
2 teaspoons icing sugar
pinch of salt
125 g unsalted butter
1 egg yolk
1½ tablespoons cold water
1 cup flaked almonds
4 sticks rhubarb,
　lightly peeled and cut
　into 6 cm × 1 cm pieces
300 ml Sugar Syrup
　(see page 23)

*Roasted quince*
3 quinces
1 cinnamon stick
500 g sugar
2 litres water

*Filling*
125 g icing sugar
2 eggs
75 g ground almonds
grated zest and juice of 1 lemon

# Tartina di cotogne e mandorle

## QUINCE TART WITH RHUBARB

To make the roasted quince, preheat the oven to 150°C. Using a heavy knife, peel the quinces and cut them in half. Remove and discard the cores and put the quince halves into a baking dish with the cinnamon stick, sugar and water. Cover with aluminium foil and bake for about 2 hours until the quince has turned a rich deep-red colour. Remove from the oven and allow to cool.

Increase the oven temperature to 180°C and grease a 35 cm × 11 cm tin with butter. Sift the flours, icing sugar and salt into a bowl. Rub in the butter until it resembles breadcrumbs, then add the egg yolk and cold water. Knead until combined. Roll out the dough and line the prepared tin. Refrigerate for 20 minutes. Line the pastry case with aluminium foil and fill with dried beans, then bake for 15 minutes. Remove the beans and bake for a further 5 minutes.

To make the filling, combine the icing sugar, eggs, ground almonds, lemon zest and lemon juice and mix well. Pour into the pastry case. Arrange the quince on top, then sprinkle with almonds and bake for 35 minutes until golden.

Meanwhile, put the rhubarb into a saucepan with the sugar syrup and bring to the boil. Reduce the heat and simmer for 10 minutes or until the rhubarb is tender. Allow to cool.

Remove the tart from the oven and allow to cool. Spoon the rhubarb onto the tart to serve.

Note: Quince and rhubarb have a 'cool weather' connotation, but you could substitute peaches, pears or berries depending on the season.

*Pannacotta isn't new, but this is an unusual way of doing it. I think buttermilk – a by-product of making butter – is lovely, with its sharpness. I love it in a dessert because it 'cleans it up' a bit. I'm not a full-on sweet tooth. I know some people love that real sugar hit, but I quite like things with some freshness as well. If you feel the same as I do about desserts, you'll like this! It requires a little technique, but once you've got the hang of it, you can make all kinds of variations and flavours. At the restaurant we like to serve it with small fritters made with roasted quince, and a lovely mint syrup. I have included instructions for making the fritters and syrup on page 192.*

# Pannacotta di siero con cotogna e menta

## BUTTERMILK PANNACOTTA WITH QUINCE JELLY AND MINT SYRUP

*Quince jelly*
3 quinces
1 cinnamon stick
500 g caster sugar
2 litres water
2 gelatine leaves
 (3 g in total)

*Buttermilk pannacotta*
4 gelatine leaves
 (7 g in total)
1 litre buttermilk
130 g caster sugar
1 vanilla bean

First, make the quince jelly. Preheat the oven to 150°C. Using a heavy knife, peel the quinces and cut them in half. Remove and discard the cores and put the quince halves into a baking dish with the cinnamon stick, sugar and water. Cover with aluminium foil and bake for about 2 hours until the quince has turned a rich deep-red colour. Remove from the oven and allow to cool. Remove 1 cup syrup from the baking dish and put it into a heavy-based saucepan. Cover and refrigerate the quince and remaining syrup. Soak the gelatine leaves in cold water for 2 minutes. Heat the 1 cup syrup gently to simmering point, then remove from the heat. Remove the gelatine leaves from the water and squeeze well. Add to the syrup and stir until dissolved. The jelly should be of a pouring consistency. Set aside.

To make the *pannacotta*, soak the gelatine leaves in cold water for 2 minutes. Put 1 cup buttermilk, the sugar and the vanilla bean into a saucepan and bring to simmering point, then remove from the heat. Remove the gelatine leaves from the water and squeeze well. Add to the milk and stir until dissolved, then allow to cool. Stir in the remaining buttermilk.

Have ready 12 × 130 ml moulds. Pour quince jelly into each mould to come about 1 cm up the sides, then refrigerate for about 30 minutes until set. Remove from the refrigerator and pour in buttermilk mixture to half fill the remaining space in the moulds. Refrigerate until set. Remove from the refrigerator and pour in quince jelly to half fill the remaining space in the moulds. Refrigerate again, then fill the moulds with buttermilk mixture. Refrigerate for several hours (preferably overnight). ▶

*Quince fritters (optional)*
1 teaspoon instant dried yeast
2 tablespoons warm milk
250 g flour
pinch of salt
175 g softened butter
reserved roasted quince
    (*see* method)
300 ml vegetable oil

*Mint syrup (optional)*
2 handfuls mint leaves
1 cup light corn syrup

Next day, if desired, make the fritters. Put the yeast and warm milk into the bowl of an electric mixer and whisk until well combined. Change the whisk attachment to a dough hook. Add the flour and salt and mix on a low speed until smooth. Add the butter a little at a time, making sure each piece is well incorporated before adding the next. Form the dough into a ball, then wrap in plastic wrap and refrigerate for 1 hour.

Meanwhile, if desired, make the mint syrup. Bring a small saucepan of water to the boil. Submerge the mint leaves in the boiling water for 10 seconds, then remove and refresh under cold running water. Squeeze well, then put into a blender. Add the corn syrup and blend well. Pass the syrup through a fine sieve into a bowl, then cover and refrigerate.

Roll out the fritter dough to a thickness of 5 mm, then cut out 36 circles 5 cm in diameter. Put a small piece of roasted quince in the centre of each circle. Wet the edge of the dough with a finger dipped in water and fold over the quince to form a half-moon shape. Press the edges firmly to seal. Heat the oil in a deep pan or a deep-fryer until hot, then fry the fritters for 3–4 minutes in batches, moving them around in the oil, until golden. Drain on kitchen paper.

To serve, put 3 fritters on each plate, turn out a buttermilk pannacotta in the centre of the plate and drizzle with the mint syrup.    *Serves 12*

*Semifreddo (meaning 'half-cold') is another Sicilian dessert. It doesn't require an ice-cream machine, but you do need a candy thermometer to measure the temperature precisely – if the water freezes, it will go rock-hard, but if it's not cold enough the mixture will remain runny and sugary. Serve the semifreddo with biscotti or crostoli (see page 179).*

# Semifreddo di favo

## HONEYCOMB SEMIFREDDO

200 g honey
80 g liquid glucose
80 g sugar
5 large egg whites
900 ml lightly whipped cream

### Honeycomb
sweet almond oil *or* other neutral oil
350 g sugar
¼ cup water
125 g liquid glucose
2½ tablespoons honey
1½ tablespoons bicarbonate of soda

To make the honeycomb, oil a deep 24 cm × 30 cm tray well and put it into the freezer. Combine the sugar, water, glucose and honey in a heavy-based saucepan and bring to the boil. Boil for 10 minutes until the mixture turns a light honey colour (reaching a temperature of about 140°C). Remove the tray from the freezer. Take the saucepan off the heat and whisk in the bicarbonate of soda, then pour the mixture into the cold tray. Return the tray to the freezer until cold. Break the honeycomb into small pieces.

Combine the honey, glucose and sugar in a heavy-based saucepan and cook over a high heat until the temperature reaches 125°C. Remove from the stove and allow to cool to 90°C. Using an electric mixer, whisk the egg whites until fluffy. With the mixer on high speed, add the cooled syrup in a gentle stream. Once it has all been incorporated, mix for a further 5 minutes on high speed. Pour the mixture into a large bowl and mix through the honeycomb. Fold in the cream, then pour into a terrine mould (or a glass or ceramic bowl, or individual moulds), and freeze overnight. The semifreddo will keep for at least 3 weeks in the freezer. *Serves 20*

Note: This recipe lends itself nicely to different flavours. In the restaurant we do it with praline, or you could try dried fruit, such as figs, for something fresher.

*The batter for these crêpes is very brown, and you can taste the chestnut flavour in them when they're cooked. The banana filling is delicious, and the chocolate sauce just finishes it off. I scatter sugar over the hot filling and caramelise it with a blowtorch, which gives the crêpes a lovely finish.*

# Crespelle di castagne con banane

## CHESTNUT-FLOUR CRÊPES WITH CARAMELISED BANANA

¾ cup plain flour
½ cup chestnut flour
   (see Note)
1 tablespoon caster sugar
4 eggs, beaten
1 cup milk
1 tablespoon melted butter
icing sugar

### Banana filling
7 bananas
1 tablespoon butter
¼ cup caster sugar
¼ cup brown sugar
¼ cup golden syrup
dash of rum (optional)
¼ cup cream

### Chocolate sauce
½ cup thickened cream
¼ cup Sugar Syrup
   (see page 23)
1 cup dark chocolate buttons

Mix the flours and sugar, then make a well in the centre and add the eggs. Gradually add the milk until the mixture coats your finger. Stir in the butter. Allow the batter to rest for 1 hour.

To make the filling, peel and slice 5 of the bananas. Melt the butter in a large frying pan, then add the caster sugar and the sliced banana. Cook over a gentle heat for 5 minutes, turning the banana, until light caramel in colour. Add the brown sugar and cook until the sugar has dissolved. Add the golden syrup and bring to a simmer. If desired, add the rum at this point. Mix in the cream, then remove the pan from the heat. The mixture should be moist but not watery. Slice the remaining bananas and add to the pan. Heat gently until warmed through.

To make the sauce, bring the cream and sugar syrup to the boil. Pour the hot liquid over the chocolate and whisk until smooth.

Grease a small frying pan with a little oil and heat gently. Pour in enough batter to coat the bottom of the pan and cook for 1 minute. Using a spatula, turn the crêpe over and cook for 30 seconds. Slide it out onto a plate and keep warm. Repeat with remaining batter.

For each diner, put 1 crêpe on a plate and spoon on some banana filling. Top with another crêpe, then dust with icing sugar. Alternatively, spoon banana filling onto each crêpe and roll up. Pour warm chocolate sauce around the crêpes and serve immediately. *Serves 6*

Note: Chestnut flour is quite common in Italian cooking, and you can buy it from old-fashioned Italian delicatessens and grocers. It's used for things like *castagnaccio*, a rich, flat cake cooked with rosemary and olive oil that is a Tuscan speciality. It's not really flour – it's ground chestnuts – so you can't replace it with plain flour in a recipe.

*Some people might think rice pudding is a bit old-fashioned, or that Marsala isn't a refined ingredient – but I think this beautiful dessert will change their minds. Rice is a very good medium when you need something as a binder, such as in this pudding. You need only a very small amount to bring it all together and hold it, and the soft, creamy texture is fantastic.*

## Budini di Marsala e riso

### MARSALA RICE PUDDINGS

2 cups milk
grated zest of 2 oranges
1 vanilla bean, split
75 g arborio rice
385 g caster sugar
5 eggs
1 candied clementine *or*
    50 g candied citrus peel,
    chopped
50 g roasted almonds,
    chopped
100 ml Marsala
    (*see* Note)

*Caramel*
200 g sugar
50 ml water

Preheat the oven to 150°C. Put the milk, orange zest, vanilla bean and rice into a heavy-based saucepan and bring to the boil. Reduce the heat to a simmer and cook for about 15 minutes, stirring every so often so that the rice does not stick to the bottom of the pot. The mixture should resemble a thick porridge. Remove from the heat and allow to cool. Using an electric mixer, beat the sugar and eggs until creamy. Add the egg mixture to the cooled rice mixture and stir. Add the clementine, almonds and Marsala and stir well.

Have ready 8 × 130 ml moulds. To make the caramel, combine the sugar and water in a heavy-based saucepan and bring to the boil over a high heat. Boil until the mixture begins to turn yellow–gold. Remove from the heat and pour a small amount of caramel into the base of each mould. Fill up with rice mixture. Put the moulds into a baking tray and bake for 40–45 minutes. Turn out immediately to serve hot. If you wish to serve the puddings cold, allow them to cool in the moulds. When ready to serve, stand the moulds in shallow, very hot water for 5–10 seconds to release the caramel base, then run a knife around the edges before turning out.   *Serves 8*

Note: In the restaurant we use a really nice, aged Sicilian Marsala, which is not overly sweet like the imitation ones we get in Australia. Real Marsala is a fortified wine named after the Sicilian town from where it was exported to England. It can be a very nice apéritif or after-dinner drink.

*The Venetians popularised chocolate in Italy. They had special shops to go to in order to drink it. Now it is a regular drink in most cafes throughout the country, but having a hot chocolate in Caffe Florian in Venice's Piazza San Marco is still a special treat. This cake is as wicked as those Venetians, and should be served with lots of double cream. It is a take on a traditional dessert, the Monte Bianco (or Mont Blanc), named after the famous snow-capped mountain on the border of France and Italy.*

# Torta di cioccolato

## FLOURLESS CHOCOLATE CAKE

900 g best-quality dark chocolate
(such as Valrhona; see Note)
180 g mascarpone
1 tablespoon Grand Marnier
1½ cups caster sugar
12 eggs
250 g tinned sweetened
chestnut purée
250 g Pastry Cream
(see page 24)

Preheat the oven to 200°C. Melt the chocolate in a large bowl over hot water or in the microwave. Combine the mascarpone and Grand Marnier in a separate bowl and set over hot water or put in the microwave to warm through. Put the sugar and eggs into the top of a double boiler and whisk over a gentle heat until thick and creamy. Stir the mascarpone mixture into the chocolate, then stir in a little of the egg mixture. Add the remaining egg mixture and mix well. Pour into a 24 cm round tin and put the tin into a baking dish. Pour in water to come two thirds up the sides of the baking dish, then transfer to the oven and bake for 30 minutes. Cover with aluminium foil and bake for a further 30 minutes. Remove from the oven and allow to cool in the tin before turning out onto a serving plate.

Put one third of the chestnut purée and half the pastry cream into a bowl. In a separate bowl, combine the remaining chestnut purée and pastry cream. Mix both bowls well. One mixture should be darker than the other. Smother the cake with the darker cream, then cover with the lighter cream allowing some of the darker cream to be visible through the lighter cream. If you wish, use a fork or the back of a spoon to tease the cream so that small peaks form, creating the look of a snow-capped mountain.

Note: This dessert is a great alternative for those on a gluten-free diet. You can do it as a large cake, which looks impressive at the table with a big mound of luscious chestnut cream and perhaps some glazed chestnuts, or as individual desserts (bake in dariole moulds for half the time given above). I always like to use high-quality chocolate in recipes, and Valrhona is one of the best. I love some of their 'single plantation' chocolates.

*This wicked and sexy little trifle (I call it* zuppa *after* zuppa inglese, *the well-known custard trifle) is made with* panettone, *the Italian Christmas cake. There always tends to be some* panettone *left over that ends up going a little stale. You can throw it out, or you can make a trifle with it.*

# Zuppa di panettone

## PANETTONE TRIFLE

1 panettone,
 cut into 5 mm slices
½ cup whisky
1 cup Sugar Syrup
 (see page 23)
4 dried figs, finely sliced
1 cup mascarpone
1 cup Pastry Cream
 (see page 24)

Select 8 × 130 ml serving glasses. Using a circle cutter, cut the panettone into circles that will fit the serving glasses. Combine the whisky with the sugar syrup, then add the dried figs.

In a separate bowl, combine the mascarpone with the pastry cream.

Put a spoonful of mascarpone mixture into each serving glass. Follow this with a spoonful of figs, then a circle of panettone. Pour some whisky syrup over so that it soaks through the panettone. Continue layering in this way until the serving glasses are full, finishing with a layer of mascarpone mixture. Refrigerate for at least 2 hours before serving. *Serves 8*

Note: *Panettone* is traditionally from the Lombardia region and has fruit and candied peel through it. I like to buy Flamigni-brand *panettone*, but there are many other good brands available at specialist food stores and supermarkets.

## Acknowledgements

Running a restaurant like Grossi Florentino, which provides food and service to clients six days a week from morning till night, takes a lot of time out of the day. Put a book like this into the mix and I can only describe the outcome as an explosion of activity. It takes many devoted people to bring a project like this to fruition.

My publisher, Julie Gibbs, is a constant inspiration and without her belief in me this project would never have got off the ground. Her input has been invaluable. Her team has also been an essential part in the crafting of this book: special thanks must go to Katie Purvis, my editor, whose patience and relentless perseverance are amazing, and Nikki Townsend, for her beautiful design work.

Once again I have teamed up with Adrian Lander and his team on photography – he is a genius with the camera and has captured the spirit of *My Italian Heart* with his incredible photographs. Thanks also to Bison Homewares Australia, Lars23 and The Essential Ingredient (Melbourne) for supplying simply gorgeous props for the shoot.

Having Mirka Mora doing illustrations for this book has been a privilege, and her enthusiasm for the project has made me proud. I first saw Mirka's work many years ago when I visited my dad at work at Tolarno, where the walls of the small dining room were adorned with her colourful drawings. I was only ten years old at the time, but you never forget such things. Her contribution has added an extra dimension to this book.

*My Italian Heart* is a snapshot of experiences – experiences in home life as well as professional life. It is a tribute to the great cooks and food-interested people I have worked with and been exposed to, from my Italian mother, Marisa, to my Spanish connection, Mira, to my Australian mother-in-law, Anne, to my Neapolitan sister-in-law, to all the passionate cooks and apprentices in the industry and everyone in between. I am continually influenced by all of you who take the time to pick up a knife or warm a *padella*. Thank you to Melissa, my wife, for her support and assistance, to my Carlo and Loredana, for putting up with me, and my sister, Elizabeth, for keeping me on my toes.

I must thank all of my staff at Grossi Florentino for their endless support, and all of my cooks for their tireless efforts. Special thanks to Pierluigi Papini, Maria Williams and Jeanette Barker – without them I would go nowhere! To Chris Rodriguez, my brother-in-law, who has worked by my side for two decades, I can say only 'Thank you' and hope that we will be together forever. The food that we craft is ours, not mine.

# Index

## a

*Agresto con mele* 30
almonds
  Almond biscuits 175
  Frangipane 24
  Lamb chops with almond and olive 99
anchovies
  Anchovy pastries 167
  Bruschetta with anchovies and capers 126
  buying 125
antipasti 28
  Apple and verjuice dressing 30
  Bresaola with prickly pear 34
  Fried calamari salad 34
  Mussels au gratin 33
  Ox tongue with salsa verde 37
  Pickled pork 37
  Preserved eggplant in oil 126
  Soused fish 33
  Stuffed calamari 109
  Swordfish terrine 29
  Tuna-filled eggs 30
appetisers 161–70
apples
  Apple and verjuice dressing 30
  Caramel apple pastries 186
artichokes 114
  Preserved artichokes in oil 128
  Roman-style artichokes 117
  Spaghettini with artichokes and olive paste 129
asiago 134
*Asparagi con prosciutto, fontina e uovo in camicia* 87
asparagus
  Asparagus with prosciutto, fontina and poached egg 87
  Roasted eggplant with porcini, asparagus and buffalo-milk mozzarella 45

## b

baccalà
  Fried baccalà balls 164
Baked fennel with gorgonzola 118
banana
  Caramelised banana 195
basic preparations 17–24
basil 16
  Basil pesto 18
  Salad of homemade pasta with tomato and basil 140
bay leaves 17
beans (dried)
  Spelt soup with beans 81
beef
  air-dried 34
  Beef stock 19
  Boiled meats with piera 97–8
  Bresaola with prickly pear 34
  choosing 12
  Kobe 12, 49
  Raw wagyu with vincotto and chicory 49
  wagyu 12, 49
*Biga* 22
*Bigoli con patate e tartufi* 62
Bigoli with potato and truffle 62
biscuits
  Almond biscuits 175
blender 10
Boiled meats with piera 97–8
*Bollito misto con piera* 97–8
*Bomboloni* 176
Bone-marrow ravioli 72
bowls 11
brains 13
Braised broad beans 115
Braised cabbage 118
Braised mussels with tomato, chilli and olives 92
Braised oxtail with tomato and red wine and braised parsnip 94
Braised parsnip 94
Braised veal shanks with lentils 103
bread
  Bruschetta with anchovies and capers 126

Crostini with duck-liver ragù 170
Focaccia with rosemary 156
homemade 152–3
Pagnotta 155
Schiacciata with grapes 156
Starter bread dough 22
Tomato crostini 43
Tuscan bread and tomato salad 56
yeast 153
bread, sweet
  Pan di San Lorenzo 158
  Panettone trifle 200
  Schiacciata all'uva 156
  Spiced bread 184
*Bresaola con fico d'India* 34
Bresaola with prickly pear 34
broad beans 114
  Braised broad beans 115
  Broad-bean ravioli with cherry tomato sauce 64
broccoli raab
  Ear-shaped pasta with broccoli raab 67
*Brodo di manzo* 19
*Brodo di pesce* 20
*Brodo di pollo* 20
*Brodo di verdura* 20
*Brodo di vitello* 19
broth
  Mushroom broth 91
*Bruschetta con acciughe e capperi* 126
Bruschetta with anchovies and capers 126
*Budini di Marsala e riso* 196
butchers 12–14
Buttermilk pannacotta with quince jelly and mint syrup 191–2

c

cabbage
  Braised cabbage 118
cake tins 11
cakes
  Flourless chocolate cake 199
  Sponge cake 180
calamari
  Calamari sauce 71
  Fried calamari salad 34
  Stuffed calamari 109
*Calamari ripieni* 109
*Cannelloni di coniglio con funghi* 69–70
*Cantuccini* 175
*Cape sante vive con soffiato di porri* 88
capers 125
  Bruschetta with anchovies and capers 126
*Carabaccia* 78
caramel 196
  Caramel apple pastries 186
  Caramelised banana 195
*Carciofi alla romana* 117
*Carciofi sotto olio* 128
*Carne con vincotto e cicoria* 49
carpaccio
  White fish carpaccio with citrus 39
*Carpaccio di pesce bianco* 39
*Cassata alla siciliana* 180
*Castagne arrosto* 150
cavolo nero 98
*Cavolo stufato* 118
*Cervo in salmì* 104
cheese
  asiago 134
  Asparagus with prosciutto, fontina and poached egg 87
  Baked fennel with gorgonzola 118
  Eggplant parmigiana 145
  Gnocchi with gorgonzola sauce 63
  Herb soup with ricotta ravioli 76
  Pizza with prosciutto and gorgonzola 154
  Roasted eggplant with porcini, asparagus and buffalo-milk mozzarella 45
  Roasted red peppers stuffed with fetta 150
  Salad of zucchini and buffalo-milk mozzarella 143
Cherry tomato sauce 64
chestnuts
  chestnut flour 195
  Chestnut-flour crêpes with caramelised banana 195
  Flourless chocolate cake 199
  Roasted chestnut and mushroom soup 82
  Roasted chestnuts 150
chicken
  Bollito misto con piera 97–8
  Chicken stock 20
  choosing 13
  Stracciatella 78
chicory
  Raw wagyu with vincotto and chicory 49
chilli
  Braised mussels with tomato, chilli and olives 92
chocolate
  Chocolate sauce 195
  Flourless chocolate cake 199
chopping boards 10
cinnamon 17
  Cinnamon ice-cream 188
*Coda di bue brasata con vino rosso* 94
colander 10
cold section of menu 27–8, 38
containers 11
contorni 114–20
coriander 16
*Cotoletta alla milanese* 142
*Cozze alla siciliana* 92
*Cozze gratinate* 33
Crab salad with pomegranate salmoriglio 40
*Crema di mandorle* 24
*Crema pasticcera* 24
crêpes
  Chestnut-flour crêpes with caramelised banana 195
*Crespelle di castagne con banane* 195
*Crocchette di baccalà* 164
*Crostini fegatini* 170
crostini
  Crostini with duck-liver ragù 170
  Tomato crostini 43
Crostoli 179
Cucumber salad 112
cured pork cheek 67

d

demi-glace 19
*Dentice in cartoccio* 108
dough
  Fresh pasta dough 21
  Pizza dough 21
  Starter bread dough 22
doughnuts
  Italian doughnuts filled with pastry cream 176
dressings
  Apple and verjuice dressing 30
  Mayonnaise 18
  Pomegranate salmoriglio 40
  Salsa verde 37
Duck pie 100
Duck-liver ragù 170

e

Ear-shaped pasta with broccoli raab 67
eggplant
  Eggplant parmigiana 145
  Preserved eggplant in oil 126
  Roasted eggplant with porcini, asparagus and buffalo-milk mozzarella 45
eggs
  Asparagus with prosciutto, fontina and poached egg 87
  Potato frittata 139
  Stracciatella 78
  Tuna-filled eggs 30
entrées 38–49
equipment 10–11

f

*Fagiano con porcini* 102
farro 81
*Fave brasate* 115
*Fegato alla veneziana* 106
fennel
  Baked fennel with gorgonzola 118
  Fennel and orange salad 51
fetta
  Roasted red peppers stuffed with fetta 150
figs
  Fig tart 185
  Spiced figs 46
Fillets of snapper baked in paper 108
*Finocchio al gorgonzola* 118

first courses
  cool 38–49
  hot 86
  *see also* pasta; salads; soups
fish
  Anchovy pastries 167
  choosing 14, 107
  farmed 13–14
  Fillets of snapper baked in paper 108
  Fish stock 20
  freshness 14
  Fried baccalà balls 164
  reef 110
  Roasted reef fish with saffron mussel sauce and red-wine risotto 110
  Roasted whole big fish 146
  smoked 29
  Soused fish 33
  Spaghetti with tuna and porcini mushrooms 130
  Swordfish rolls with pine nuts and sultanas 113
  Swordfish terrine 29
  tinned 30, 125
  Tuna sandwiches 167
  Tuna-filled eggs 30
  White fish carpaccio with citrus 39
fishmongers 14
flan rings 11
Flourless chocolate cake 199
*Focaccia al rosmarino* 156
Focaccia with rosemary 156
foie gras
  availability 46
  Rabbit and foie gras terrine with spiced figs 46
fontina
  Asparagus with prosciutto, fontina and poached egg 87
food processor 10
Frangipane 24
Fresh pasta dough 21
Fried baccalà balls 164
Fried calamari salad 34
Fried prawn salad 140
frittata
  Potato frittata 139
*Frittata di patate* 139

fritters
  Quince fritters 192
frozen desserts *see* iced desserts
fruit suppliers 14–16

g

game
  farmed 13
  Pheasant with porcini sauce 102
  Roasted quail with mushroom broth 91
  roasting 93
  Venison stew 104
glazes
  Orange glaze 180
gnocchi 60
  Gnocchi with gorgonzola sauce 63
*Gnocchi gorgonzola* 63
gorgonzola
  Baked fennel with gorgonzola 118
  Gnocchi with gorgonzola sauce 63
  Pizza with prosciutto and gorgonzola 154
  types 63
grapes
  Schiacciata with grapes 156
graters 10
greengrocers 14–15
Grilled scampi with cucumber salad 112
grinders 10
guinea fowl 102

h

herbs
  choosing 15
  Herb soup with ricotta ravioli 76
  *see also* particular herbs
honey
  Honeycomb semifreddo 193
  Saffron honey pears 179

i

iced desserts
  *Cassata alla siciliana* 180
  Cinnamon ice-cream 188
  Honeycomb semifreddo 193

Saffron ice-cream 188
Spiced ice-cream terrine with spiced bread and red-wine syrup 183–4
Star anise ice-cream 188
*Insalata di calamari* 34
*Insalata di finocchio e arancia* 51
*Insalata di funghi* 54
*Insalata di gamberi* 140
*Insalata di granchio* 40
*Insalata di patate e cavolrape* 52
*Insalata di pomodoro e cipolla* 54
*Insalata di zucchini con mozzarella di bufalo* 143
intermezzo 161–70
*Involtini di pesce spada* 113
Italian doughnuts filled with pastry cream 176
Italian fried potatoes 120

j

jelly
  Quince jelly 191
juicer 10

k

kitchen space 9, 17
kitchen tools 10–11
knives 10
Kobe beef 12, 49
kohlrabi
  Potato and kohlrabi salad 52

l

lamb
  choosing 12–13
  Lamb chops with almond and olive 99
Leek soufflés 88
leftovers 86
lentils
  Braised veal shanks with lentils 103
  Lentil soup with pork sausage 75
*Lingua di bue in salsa verde* 37
Live giant Tasmanian scallops with leek soufflés 88

liver
  Pan-fried calf's liver with onions and white wine 106

m

*Maiale salmistrato* 37
main courses 85–113
*Maionese* 18
Marsala rice puddings 196
Mayonnaise 18
measuring jugs 10
meat
  ageing 93
  choosing 12–14, 93
  cuts 93
  *see also* beef; game; lamb; offal; pork; veal
*Melanzane alla parmigiana* 145
*Melanzane con porcini, asparagi e mozzarella di bufalo* 45
*Melanzane sotto olio* 126
mincer 10–11
*Minestra di farro* 81
mint 16
  Mint syrup 192
mixing bowls 11
mortar and pestle 10
mouli 10
mozzarella 45
  Roasted eggplant with porcini, asparagus and buffalo-milk mozzarella 45
  Salad of zucchini and buffalo-milk mozzarella 143
mushrooms
  dried 45, 125
  frozen 45
  Mushroom broth 91
  Mushroom salad 54
  Porcini sauce 102
  Risotto with porcini mushrooms 132
  Roasted chestnut and mushroom soup 82
  Roasted eggplant with porcini, asparagus and buffalo-milk mozzarella 45
  Spaghetti with tuna and porcini mushrooms 130

Wild mushroom sauce 69–70
mussels
   Braised mussels with tomato, chilli and olives 92
   Mussels au gratin 33
   opening 33
   Saffron mussel sauce 110
myrtle 16

## n

non-stick pans 11
nutmeg 17

## o

Octopus terrine with tomato crostini 43
offal
   Boiled meats with piera 97–8
   brains 13
   Braised oxtail with tomato and red wine and braised parsnip 94
   choosing 13
   cured pork cheek 67
   ox cheek 98
   Ox tongue with salsa verde 37
   Pan-fried calf's liver with onions and white wine 106
   sweetbreads 13
   tripe 13
olives
   Braised mussels with tomato, chilli and olives 92
   Lamb chops with almond and olive 99
   olive paste 99
   Spaghettini with artichokes and olive paste 129
   storing 125
   varieties 129
olive oil 124
   Spaghetti with garlic and olive oil 132
onions
   Pan-fried calf's liver with onions and white wine 106
   Tomato and onion salad 54
   Tuscan onion soup 78
oranges
   Fennel and orange salad 51
   Orange glaze 180
*Orecchiette con cime di rapa* 67
ox cheek 98
Ox tongue with salsa verde 37
oxtail
   Braised oxtail with tomato and red wine and braised parsnip 94
   choosing 13
oysters
   Apple and verjuice dressing 30

## p

*Pagnotta* 155
*Pan di San Lorenzo* 158
Panettone trifle 200
Pan-fried calf's liver with onions and white wine 106
Pan-fried crumbed veal 142
pannacotta
   Buttermilk pannacotta with quince jelly and mint syrup 191–2
*Pannacotta di siero con cotogna e menta* 191–2
pans 11
pantry staples 123–5
*Panzanella* 56
parsley 15–16
parsnip
   Braised parsnip 94
pasta
   Bigoli with potato and truffle 62
   Bone-marrow ravioli 72
   Broad-bean ravioli with cherry tomato sauce 64
   cooking 61
   cutting 21, 62
   dry 60–1, 124
   Ear-shaped pasta with broccoli raab 67
   Fresh pasta dough 21
   Gnocchi with gorgonzola sauce 63
   making 21, 59, 60
   Penne matriciana 130
   Rabbit cannelloni with wild mushroom sauce 69–70
   Ricotta ravioli 76
   Salad of homemade pasta with tomato and basil 140
   Spaghetti with garlic and olive oil 132
   Spaghetti with tuna and porcini mushrooms 130
   Spaghettini with artichokes and olive paste 129
   Tagliarini with calamari sauce 71
*Pasta di casa in insalata* 140
*Pasta fresca* 21, 60–1
*Pasta frolla* 23
pasta machine 11
*Pasta sfoglia* 22
pastries
   Anchovy pastries 167
   Caramel apple pastries 186
   Crostoli 179
   *see also* pies; tarts
pastry
   blind-baking 23
   freezing 100, 186
   leftover 22, 100, 167
   Puff pastry 22
   Shortcrust pastry 23
pastry brush 11
Pastry cream 24
*Patate fritte* 120
pears
   Saffron honey pears 179
*Penne matriciana* 130
*Peperoni ripieni di fetta* 150
*Pere al zafferano* 179
*Pesce arrosto* 146
*Pesce arrosto con zafferano e risotto al vino rosso* 110
*Pesce in scapece* 33
*Pesto di basilico* 18
Pheasant with porcini sauce 102
pickled ox tongue 98
Pickled pork 37
Piera 97–8
pies
   Duck pie 100
   Pumpkin pie 163
piping bag 11
pizza
   making 21
   Pizza dough 21
   Pizza with prosciutto and gorgonzola 154
*Pizza al prosciutto e gorgonzola* 154
polenta
   Polenta 23
   varieties 124
*Pomegranate salmoriglio* 40
*Porcellino al forno* 149
Porcini sauce 102
pork
   choosing 12
   cured pork cheek 67
   Pickled pork 37
   Roast suckling pig 149
potato ricer 10
potatoes
   Bigoli with potato and truffle 62
   Gnocchi with gorgonzola sauce 63
   Italian fried potatoes 120
   Potato and kohlrabi salad 52
   Potato frittata 139
   for salads 52
pots 11
prawns
   Fried prawn salad 140
preserves 125
   Preserved artichokes in oil 128
   Preserved eggplant in oil 126
prickly pear
   Bresaola with prickly pear 34
prosciutto
   Asparagus with prosciutto, fontina and poached egg 87
   Pizza with prosciutto and gorgonzola 154
Puff pastry 22
Pumpkin pie 163

## q

*Quaglie arrosto con brodo di funghi* 91
quail
   Roasted quail with mushroom broth 91
quinces
   Quince fritters 192
   Quince jelly 191
   Quince tart with rhubarb 188
   Roasted quince 188

## r

rabbit
  farmed 14, 46
  Rabbit and foie gras terrine with spiced figs 46
  Rabbit cannelloni with wild mushroom sauce 69–70
radicchio 51
ragù
  Duck-liver ragù 170
  Veal ragù 168
*Ravioli di fave con pomodorini* 64
*Ravioli di midollo* 72
Raw wagyu with vincotto and chicory 49
red peppers
  Roasted red peppers stuffed with fetta 150
Red-wine risotto 110
Red-wine syrup 184
rhubarb
  Quince tart with rhubarb 188
rice 124–5, 174
  Marsala rice puddings 196
  Rice balls filled with veal ragù 168
  *see also* risotto
ricotta
  *Cassata alla siciliana* 180
  Ricotta ravioli 76
risotto
  Red-wine risotto 110
  rice for 124–5
  Risotto with porcini mushrooms 132
  Savoury strawberry risotto 134
*Risotto con le fragole* 134
*Risotto con porcini* 132
Roast suckling pig 149
Roasted chestnut and mushroom soup 82
Roasted chestnuts 150
Roasted eggplant with porcini, asparagus and buffalo-milk mozzarella 45
Roasted quail with mushroom broth 91
Roasted quince 188
Roasted red peppers stuffed with fetta 150
Roasted reef fish with saffron mussel sauce and red-wine risotto 110
Roasted whole big fish 146
roasting trays 11
Roman-style artichokes 117
rosemary 16
  Focaccia with rosemary 156

## s

saffron 16, 174
  Saffron honey pears 179
  Saffron ice-cream 188
  Saffron mussel sauce 110
sage 16
salads 50
  Crab salad with pomegranate salmoriglio 40
  Cucumber salad 112
  Fennel and orange salad 51
  Fried calamari salad 34
  Mushroom salad 54
  Potato and kohlrabi salad 52
  Salad of homemade pasta with tomato and basil 140
  Salad of zucchini and buffalo-milk mozzarella 143
  Tomato and onion salad 54
  Tuscan bread and tomato salad 56
salmon roe 40
*Salsa di pomodoro* 18
Salsa verde 37
sandwiches
  Tuna sandwiches 167
sauces, savoury
  Calamari sauce 71
  Cherry tomato sauce 64
  demi-glace 19
  Gorgonzola sauce 63
  Porcini sauce 102
  Saffron mussel sauce 110
  Tomato sauce 18
  Wild mushroom sauce 69–70
sauces, sweet
  Caramel apple 186
  Chocolate 195
sausages
  Lentil soup with pork sausage 75
  salsiccie 75
Savoury strawberry risotto 134
scales 10
scallops
  Live giant Tasmanian scallops with leek soufflés 88
scampi 112
  Grilled scampi with cucumber salad 112
*Scampi alla piastra con cetriolo* 112
*Schiacciata all'uva* 156
Schiacciata with grapes 156
*Sciroppo* 23
scissors 11
*Scotta ditto all'olivo* 99
scrapers 10
seafood 107
  Apple and verjuice dressing 30
  Braised mussels with tomato, chilli and olives 92
  Crab salad with pomegranate salmoriglio 40
  Fried calamari salad 34
  Grilled scampi with cucumber salad 112
  Live giant Tasmanian scallops with leek soufflés 88
  Marinated fried prawns 140
  Mussels au gratin 33
  Octopus terrine with tomato crostini 43
  Saffron mussel sauce 110
  Stuffed calamari 109
  Tagliarini with calamari sauce 71
*Semifreddo di favo* 193
*Sfoglia all'acciuga* 167
*Sformato di coniglio con fichi* 46
Shortcrust pastry 23
side dishes
  Baked fennel with gorgonzola 118
  Braised broad beans 115
  Braised cabbage 118
  Italian fried potatoes 120
  Roman-style artichokes 117
sieves 10
snacks 161–70
snapper
  Fillets of snapper baked in paper 108
  Roasted whole big fish 146
soufflé
  Leek soufflés 88
soups 59–60, 74
  Herb soup with ricotta ravioli 76
  Lentil soup with pork sausage 75
  Roasted chestnut and mushroom soup 82
  Spelt soup with beans 81
  Stracciatella 78
  Tuscan onion soup 78
  *see also* stock
Soused fish 33
spaghetti
  Spaghetti with garlic and olive oil 132
  Spaghetti with tuna and porcini mushrooms 130
  Spaghettini with artichokes and olive paste 129
*Spaghetti aglio e olio* 132
*Spaghetti alla carrettiera* 130
*Spaghettini con carciofi e olive* 129
spatulas 10
Spelt soup with beans 81
spices 16–17
  Spiced bread 184
  Spiced figs 46
  Spiced ice-cream terrine with spiced bread and red-wine syrup 183–4
Sponge cake 180
spoons 10
star anise 17
  Star anise ice-cream 188
Starter bread dough 22
stew
  Venison stew 104
*Stinco di vitello con lenticchie* 103
stock 74
  Beef stock 19
  Chicken stock 20
  clarifying 98
  Fish stock 20
  Veal stock 19
  Vegetable stock 20
storage containers 11
Stracciatella 78
strawberries
  Savoury strawberry risotto 134
Stuffed calamari 109
Sugar syrup 23
*Suppli di riso al ragù* 168

suppliers 11–15
sweetbreads 13
swordfish
   Swordfish rolls with pine nuts and sultanas 113
   Swordfish terrine 29
syrup
   Mint syrup 192
   Red-wine syrup 184
   Sugar syrup 23

## t

Tagliarini with calamari sauce 71
*Tagliarini con sugo di calamari* 71
*Tartina di cotogne e mandorle* 188
tart cases 11
tarts
   Fig tart 185
   Quince tart with rhubarb 188
*Terrina di gelato alle spezie con pane alle spezie e sciroppo di vino* 183–4
*Terrina di pesce spada* 29
*Terrina di polipo con crostini di pomodoro* 43
terrines
   Octopus terrine with tomato crostini 43
   Rabbit and foie gras terrine with spiced figs 46
   Spiced ice-cream terrine with spiced bread and red-wine syrup 183–4
   Swordfish terrine 29
thermometers 11
tomatoes
   Braised mussels with tomato, chilli and olives 92
   Braised oxtail with tomato and red wine and braised parsnip 94
   Cherry tomato sauce 64
   Salad of homemade pasta with tomato and basil 140
   tinned 125
   Tomato and onion salad 54
   Tomato crostini 43
   Tomato sauce 18
   Tuscan bread and tomato salad 56
*Torta di anatra* 100
*Torta di cioccolato* 199
*Torta di fichi* 185
*Torta di zucca* 163
*Tortine di mele* 186
*Tramezzetti con tonno* 167
trays 11
trifle
   Panettone trifle 200
tripe 13
truffles
   Bigoli with potato and truffle 62
tuna
   Spaghetti with tuna and porcini mushrooms 130
   tinned 30, 125
   Tuna sandwiches 167
   Tuna-filled eggs 30
Tuscan bread and tomato salad 56
Tuscan onion soup 78

## u

*Uova tonnate* 30

## v

vanilla pods 17
veal
   Braised veal shanks with lentils 103
   choosing 13, 14
   Pan-fried crumbed veal 142
   Veal ragù 168
   Veal stock 19
vegetables
   side dishes 114–20
   suppliers 14–15
   Vegetable stock 20
   *see also* particular vegetables
Venison stew 104
verjuice
   Apple and verjuice dressing 30
vincotto
   availability 40
   Raw wagyu with vincotto and chicory 49

## w

wagyu beef 12, 49
whisks 10
White fish carpaccio with citrus 39
Wild mushroom sauce 69–70
wine
   Braised oxtail with tomato and red wine and braised parsnip 94
   Pan-fried calf's liver with onions and white wine 106
   Red-wine risotto 110
   Red-wine syrup 184
wire racks 10
workspace 9, 17

## z

zucchini
   Salad of zucchini and buffalo-milk mozzarella 143
*Zuppa di castagne arrosto e funghi* 82
*Zuppa di erbe con ravioli* 76
*Zuppa di lenticchie con salsiccie* 75
*Zuppa di panettone* 200

Go into the kitchen and cook for someone you love. The pleasure will be mine.

Guy Grossi